How to Devel

Maintain Quality

Published by
Lotus Press

Published by
Lotus Press

How to Develop and Maintain Quality

Michael E. Allen

4263/3, Ansari Road,
Darya Ganj, New Delhi-110002

LOTUS PRESS
4263/3, Ansari Road, Darya Ganj, New Delhi-110002
Ph: 30903912, 23290047, E-mail: lotus_press@sify.com

HOW TO DEVELOP AND MAINTAIN QUALITY
ISBN 81-8382-016-6

Published by: Lotus Press, New Delhi-110002
Lasertypeset by: Reliable Infomedia, New Delhi-110009
Printed at: Gyan Sagar, New Delhi

PREFACE

In business, 'quality' is much more than a word to describe how good your product or service is — it is a broad term, covering a whole range of important systems and disciplines. Quality improvement is integral to running a business in smart way. The best organisations have a systemic and comprehensive focus on quality and performance improvement that applies to all areas of product and service, to all areas of the organisation and to all people within the organisation. This focus is not just a programme, but a way of life, a strategy requiring improvement by everybody in everything all the time and pursuing a vision of everyone doing the right things.

Quality can give the business a competitive edge and can help you to keep and gain more customers. It is important for you to have the right attitude towards quality in your business. You may want to look at using some form of outside confirmation of the quality of what you do. This book will help you workout how to improve the quality of the business. It provides all information needed by you about quality—how to achieve it, how to measure it, how to develop it and how to maintain it. It explores all aspects of quality, from quality of goods and services to the processes that are necessary to develop and maintain quality.

Editor

In business, 'quality' is much more than a word to describe how good your product or service is — it is a broad term, covering a whole range of important systems and disciplines. Quality improvement is integral to running a business in smart way. Quality can give the business a competitive edge and can help you to keep and gain more customers. It is important for you to have the right attitude towards quality in your business. You may want to look at using some form of outside confirmation of the quality of what you do.

This book will help you workout how to improve the quality of the business. It provides all information needed by you about quality—how to achieve it, how to measure it, how to develop it and how to maintain it. It explores all aspects of quality, from quality of goods and services to the processes that are necessary to develop and maintain quality.

CONTENTS

1

UNDERSTANDING QUALITY

Quality is defined as meeting or exceeding the needs and expectations of the customer. Thus, the goal of a business should be to find out what the customer wants and then fine tune the process to ensure that they get it. The primary dimensions of product quality include:

1. Performance
2. Features
3. Reliability
4. Conformance
5. Durability
6. Serviceability
7. Aesthetics
8. Perceived Quality

However, increasingly service quality is attracting equal or more attention.

1. Responsiveness
2. Reliability
3. Accuracy
4. Knowledge of Employees
5. Courtesy

6. Consistency

7. Speed

These listed dimensions of product and service quality are, in a broad sense, generic to most situations. However, every business is unique, and if customer satisfaction measurements are to be meaningful, expectations should be phrased in the language of customers for each distinct market segment. Also, some needs are more critical than others and it is wise to determine the relative importance of each need. After measuring satisfaction levels, emphasis can then be placed on improving performance in areas important to the customer but where the organisation may be lacking in comparison to the quality delivered by competitors.

1.1. CONTINUOUS QUALITY IMPROVEMENT

Continuous quality improvement begins by identifying customer expectations for all key "moments of truth" - the critical interactions customers have with the organisation. This can include contact with, for example, internal support groups, collection individuals, sales representatives, management, or direct service providers. The best way to understand customer expectations is to listen to customers using qualitative research techniques. This usually requires skillful probing by someone practiced in customer satisfaction measurement.

After identifying expectations, customer satisfaction can readily be measured. However, this requires the customer to answer specific questions about how he or she feels about the company's performance. This is why it is so important to capture their interest and build the credibility needed to gain their cooperation. The task is made considerably easier by speaking the customer's language and presenting only issues that are truly significant.

1.2. MEASURING QUALITY

More and more, quality is being measured. Companies are coming to the conclusion that if they can measure it, they can manage it and, consequently, can improve it. The best performing organisations are allowing customer expectations to drive their quality initiative. They recognise customers define quality by judging them in relation to competitors.

Organisations that constantly measure themselves in relation to competitors (Benchmarking) are able to quickly capitalise on their emerging strengths and address weaknesses before they become problems.

1.2.1. Quality Line

The quality line is an overlooked concept by many businesses. By focusing on this simple concept you may gain competitive advantage and improve your bottom line. Every business must make a decision where to put the quality line – high, low, or somewhere in-between. Where this line is placed can determine success or failure. Here are some important considerations when looking at your business' quality line:

1. Determine what your customers want and need. These wants and needs change continually and need to be monitored continually. This is the first and most important step!

2. Determine where your current quality line is. Be honest. Get objective opinions from your customers, employees and vendors.

3. Look at the gap between status quo and what is wanted and needed by your customers. This step alone may give you a great competitive advantage.

4. Make an action plan to reduce the gap. Be sure to include resources needed and costs in your plan.

Are your customers willing to pay more for the quality you provide?

5. Determine your competitor's quality line. What results are they getting? Are they giving you an opportunity to take their market share?

6. In general, the higher the quality the higher the cost. Make certain that before adding costs you will be certain of perceived value. Simply increasing costs can produce negative results for your bottom line.

7. Be especially aware of ways to improve quality with little or no cost. Since your people are your best resource here it makes good business sense to get regular input from employees. Track this input to give credibility to your focus on quality.

8. Look both inside and outside your industry for ways to improve quality. This means you are always in the 'hunt' for new ideas.

9. Reward your people for coming up with ways to improve quality. Incentives and recognition work well here.

10. Constantly balance the costs versus quality equation in your business. With the business world changing so rapidly you can quickly be left behind. By monitoring your quality line you may find different ways to compete on price.

The traditional paradigm for the life cycle of a business calls for the business owner to constantly strive to grow the business. Bigger (and busier) is supposed to equate to more profits, therefore being "better". But that's not necessarily so. For small business owners, the bottom line is not the only measurement of success, as running a successful small business is not the only important feature of our lives. We need to achieve work life balance to have a true quality of life.

When you're running a successful small business, the business seems to have a life of its own, and it's too easy to get completely enmeshed in its momentum - especially as so many successful small business owners are determined, driven types who are used to constantly striving to do more and have more. But paradoxically, when it comes to quality of life, having more can mean doing less, business-wise.

1.3. MANAGEMENT QUALITY

Management Quality is an organisational concept, which describes the organisation's capacity to meet high quality objectives in its management functions. This leads to better customer satisfaction and financial and other performance. By defining Management Quality as an organisational concept and applying established Quality methodology to the area of management, a great potential for improvement becomes apparent. This improvement translates directly to business results or other major objectives.

A model of Management Quality has been developed, and used in practice to benchmark management quality in more than ten Scandinavian and international organisations. The results clearly show that even the leading edge companies can take great steps forward, by using a structural approach to management quality and by learning from best practices of others. Practically all management development is aimed at individuals. Many enterprises and organisations have programmes for Total Quality Management. These are supposed to cover management quality, as one of several topics.

In practice, however, improvements in this area are often given a lower priority, than within processes, more directly concerning flows of products and money. To apply quality concepts and methods to the area of management includes measuring present level of quality, establishing the desired goal and necessary actions, and finally measuring progress. It is not sufficient to address the symptoms, the obvious deficiencies; you must also consider the fundamental values, policies, systems, processes and programmes, i.e. quality assurance. Management quality is not synonymous with Quality management. Nor is it synonymous with Quality of managers.

The prerequisites to obtain substantial and lasting improvements of management quality are top management determination, time and perseverance.

1. Benchmarking of management quality is a structured comparison with other leading organisations. This process identifies strengths and weaknesses and allows you to learn from the best practices of others. It is an excellent starting point for decisions about ambition and priorities in the continued improvement project(s). This is an ambitious approach, recommended if you believe that you are about to start a long-term development project.

2. A more traditional approach is to start such projects already identified or in plan (e.g. management policy, management review, and management development), but in such a manner that each project becomes a building block, that fits with the other blocks. Some kind of architecture is necessary. The model for management quality, used for benchmarking, can be very useful as a master drawing.

3. If you don't wish to use an "architecture", but still desire quality assurance of ongoing or planned projects (in the management area), the relevant

sections of the management quality model may be used. A "consultant" (internal or external) who is independent in relation to the project should carry out the quality assurance.

Communication is the key word in all stages of a project aimed at improving Management Quality. The key issue at the start is the involvement of top management. The self-assessment, made by top management is often an excellent way to show what is meant by management quality and the potential for improvement. The result of the self-assessment can be made the starting point of a management meeting or seminar, with the objective to reach an agreement if and how to proceed with benchmarking or other ways to improve management quality. There are other ways to make the decision, but the management committee (or corresponding group) must support the decision - this is the group which, as a next step, has to commit to future plans and actions.

Middle Management: The middle manager - the manager of managers - is the main implementer of Management Quality. She/he is responsible for identification of new management potential, development of those candidates, appointment of new managers, introduction and continuous development of managers, and, if necessary, the phase-out of inadequate managers. The middle manager rarely receives any education or other support to fulfil these responsibilities. It may be your first priority to set up such education for middle managers.

1.4. PRODUCTS AND SERVICES QUALITY IMPROVEMENT

Quality can give the business a competitive edge and can help you to keep and gain more customers. It is important for you to have the right attitude towards quality in your business. You may want to look at using some form of outside confirmation of the quality of what you do - for example, through ISO 9000 or Investors in People. This unit will help you work out how to improve the quality of the business or work towards these quality awards. When you improve the quality of your products and services, you will need to do the following.

— Review quality in the business.

— Decide how to improve quality in the business.

— Make sure the actions you take to improve quality help the business.

You will need to gather a range of information to be able to improve the quality of your products and services. This could include:

— Notes about the quality issues you have thought about;

— A review of how you could put them into practice in the business; or

— A review of the costs and benefits of putting them into practice.

The information might also include your early ideas about the following.

— How you will describe quality procedures and record what happens.

— How you will explain what you expect people to do and when.

— How you will describe tasks and processes.

The quality targets you consider will need to reflect the needs of the business, for example, if you are making a range of products, you may need to look at quality targets for each one. Even if the business is mainly based on providing a service to customers, you will still need to decide how you will keep a check on the quality of what you offer. When you have improved the quality of your products and services, you will probably have one or more of the following.

— A quality policy for the business.

— A quality section for the business plan.

— Clear instructions for staff about what to do to maintain quality.

Make sure you gather information on quality from all those involved in the business, using outside advice if you need it.

— Find out what your competitors do about quality.

— Find out how pleased your customers are by the level of quality you have set.

You need to know and understand the following.

— What quality management is and how you can bring it into the business

— How quality helps the business aims and targets.

— How to explain what quality and quality management are to those people involved

— What different ways there are of bringing quality into the business, and how to decide which is best for the business.

Looking at the business activities to improve quality: What information from your own business is useful when looking at quality

— How to measure quality.

— Where you can get information about quality and quality systems.

— How you can find out what your customers expect in relation to quality.

— How you can find out about what your competitors do about quality.

How to keep up to date with new opportunities and threats, and what they are likely to be. This could include:

1.5. IMPROVING YOUR BUSINESS QUALITATIVELY

Every business venture—whether a one-man operation, large corporation, or business within a business—can follow simple steps to improve. First it is necessary to have a vision or idea of what to improve. Then there are steps to follow, including measurement, organising, reducing costs and getting more customers. Questions you may have are:

— What does "improvement" mean?

— What do these steps entail?

— What are some example?

Business improvement means to move forward from the present situation. That could mean to increase profits, reduce losses, get more customers, expand the markets, become more visible in the community, go public or a number of other items deemed desirable. To improve, you must have a vision of what you want to achieve, where you want to go, and what you want the business to become.

If you, as a business leader, have an idea or vision of an area to improve, you can set that process in motion by following five steps.

1.5.1. Measure Where You are

Although you can get a "gut feeling" that your business is improving, the only real way to verify it is by some valid means of measurement. This is done both before and after some improvement effort. Measurement criteria must be real and hard, based on money or return-on-investment (ROI). Measurements of such things as customer satisfaction are soft measurements and may or may not lead to better profits. That is not to say you should measure such items, but there must be a definite, measurable correlation between it and monetary gain.

1.5.2. Organise Operations

By organising or re-organising your operations and processes, you can make your business a more effective machine. This includes defining your goals, planning, and using the ISO 9000 standards. Some companies consider making a new organisation chart (org chart) a way to re-organise their business. All that really seems to happen is that the same people are doing the same work, but now they have different titles. New organisation charts are a standard joke in the business world.

1.5.3. Reduce Costs

By using Total Quality Management (TQM) methods and tools, as well as other similar concepts, you can reduce wasted material, effort, and time in making, selling, and delivering your product. The result is an improvement in the company's bottom line and an increased competitive advantage. Since TQM became popular in the early 1990s, there have been a number of similar initiatives such as re-engineering, six sigma, and such. Some have been successful and some disastrous. Common sense and good business practice is the most important thing in applying these concepts.

1.5.4. Get More Customers

By satisfying your customers with high quality products and extra service, you will get repeat business and referrals. Of course, your price must be competitive, and they must have easy access to your product. Although marketing and advertising are important to get more customers, quality, service and customer satisfaction are what keep a business successful in the long run.

1.5.5. Measure Again

Measure again to verify your improvement. Improvement can be done in all forms of business. Following are some examples.

A computer consultant wants to improve his one-person business to get more clients. He can determine how much he is making per hour of work, how effective his advertising is, and some other measurements of where his business has been. By organising his business and how he works, he can be more efficient. This will allow him more time to spend on marketing his services. He can tune his processes to reduce wasted time and errors made. By concentrating on quality, he can improve customer satisfaction and get referrals. Finally, after a period of time, he can re-measure his criteria to see if his business has improved.

A manager of a department in a large corporation wants to improve the output and reduce employee turnover. He measures the output, turnover and how it effects the profits for his department. The company is ISO 9000 certified, so he uses the Quality Manual to help solidify his organisation. He works on improving work processes and addressing worker issues to reduce costs and losses from workers leaving or making careless mistakes.

His customer base is fixed within the company, so he tries to satisfy them through better communications. Finally, after implementing these changes, he measures his department's effectiveness again to verify the improvement.

2

HOW TO IMPROVE THE
QUALITY OF MY BUSINESS

Quality is defined as meeting customer needs. Therefore
the way to improve quality is to figure out who is the
customer and what they need, and then improve the
process to fully meet this need. There are various
techniques for doing this. They involve setting up teams
to analyse problems with the process and implement
solutions. Because the supplier is part of the process some
techniques involve teaming with the supplier to improve
the quality of incoming products.

2.1. CONCEPTS OF QUALITY MANAGEMENT

Quality management techniques and philosophies is
generally referred to as total quality management. The
core concepts are:

1. Continuous process improvement.

2. Customer focus.

3. Defect prevention.

4. Universal responsibility.

2.1.1. Continuous Process Improvement

The first step in quality improvement is for people to look

at their work in terms of being part of a continuous process. Continuous Improvement is the term used to describe the fact that process improvement takes place in incremental steps. It never stops. However good things may be, they can always be better. Continuous improvement is a relentless effort to add value for the customer. The steps in the Continuous Improvement process are to:

1. Select an improvement project with a specific goal.
2. Assign a team to improve it.
3. Define the process using a flow chart.
4. Define variability and problems in the process.
5. Find the root causes of the problems.
6. Recommend improvements.
7. Implement the improvements as a pilot project.
8. Measure the results.
9. Proceed to a final implementation.
10. Move on to the next problem.

The continuous improvement process should be driven from the top, but implemented from the bottom. The selection of improvement projects needs a sharp focus. The problem areas must be prioritised, critical processes selected for improvement, and improvement goals set for the project team. This is a top down process. There are various techniques which teams can use for their quality improvement work. Training must be provided so that the teams know how to use these techniques:

1. Processes are described using flow charts.
2. Problem solving is done using system failure analysis, cause/effect analysis and brainstorming.
3. Customer needs may be defined using a Quality Function Deployment Matrix.

4. Processes are monitored using statistical process control techniques.

5. Inventory control and supplier management techniques are used to improve the inputs.

Staff who are assigned to project improvement teams need to understand how to use these techniques. Managers and supervisors need to understand these techniques too, because it is their job to facilitate and drive the quality improvement effort.

2.1.2. Customer Focus

Everyone has a customer. The external customer is the person who purchases the product or service. We also have to think of the internal customers. Internal customers are those who use what another group provides. This has quite profound implications. It means that every work group has to think about providing value to the people who use their product. This involves finding out exactly what the user needs and wants, and ensuring that the process provides it. The starting point for quality improvement is to determine the customer needs. When the needs are fairly simple, this can be done merely by talking to them.

When one is dealing with an external customer and the product is very complex, the determination of the customer needs can be quite time consuming and requires a detailed analysis. A useful tool for determining the customer needs and ensuring that these needs are incorporated into the product design is the Quality Function Deployment Matrix. Determining customer needs accurately is an important aspect of quality control. Obviously, it is less costly to rectify a mistake in defining customer requirements before a product is produced than it is afterwards. So spending the time and effort to figure out the requirements correctly at the start is time well spent.

2.1.3. Defect Prevention

Defect prevention saves money. Imagine a process for manufacturing a product. It begins with a specification. Drawings are produced, parts are made and assembled, and the product is delivered to the customer. The cost of rectifying a defect increases by at least a factor of ten as the product moves through each of these stages. Defect prevention is concerned with catching the errors as early in the game as possible or preventing them from occurring at all.

2.1.4. Universal Responsibility

This concept deals with the fact that quality is not only the responsibility of the inspection department but is everyone's responsibility. Quality should be totally pervasive. Every work group in the business should be concerned with seeking ways to improve the quality of their own product or service.

2.2. TECHNIQUES TO IMPROVE QUALITY MANAGEMENT

There are a number of management approaches and techniques which have been developed to support these four core concepts. These are:

2.2.1. Statistics for Process Control

Quality control is based on using statistical analysis to measure and predict the performance of processes. One must have a rudimentary understanding of statistics to appreciate the thinking that goes in to process control. Statistics is a fairly intimidating branch of mathematics that deals with variability. It is quite complex and very few people have training in the subject. However some of the ideas that apply to process control can be explained easily enough without resorting to the mathematics. Statistics deals with variability. It is used to predict and control the performance of a system based on measurements of the output from the system.

The point about variability is that whenever you take a group of measurements you will almost always get a bell shaped, normal distribution curve. Any group of measurements exhibits variability which can be described in statistical terms. Because of this characteristic we are able use statistical methods to monitor and control processes. We do this by taking samples from the output of a process, measuring them, plotting them and interpreting the resulting graph. This allow us to see whether the process is under control. It provides indications about how it can be fixed, if necessary. Although statistical process control is usually applied to production processes it can also be applied to non production processes. The key is to measure the critical variables in the process and then to monitor them for signs of impending problems.

Tracking is done using a process control chart. Samples are taken from the output and plotted on the chart. The chart shows how the output varies over time. What the chart tells you is whether the variability in output is due to normal variation or whether there are special causes present. To improve the process one first attempts to eliminate the special causes, so that the variations are only due to the normal random factors.

Once the process is under control and the special causes have been eliminated, one can only make further improvements by improving the process. The improvement goals will either be to reduce the variation or to reduce the absolute value of the factor being measured. Typically, for a production process the goal will be to tighten up on the tolerances so no defects are produced. For an administrative function or service process, the improvement goal will likely be to cut down the cycle time or to reduce the cost of the process.

2.2.2. Involvement and Empowerment of an Employee

Involvement means that management actively encourages involvement in running the operation and improving the processes. Empowerment is something more. It means that management recognises that when staff are given training and provided with the right information, they are in the best position to control their own work processes. This being the case, they should be empowered to do it. There are various techniques to solicit employee involvement. Suggestion schemes work well when they are well publicised and when worthwhile rewards are provided. The job design can be improved to be more satisfying. Continuous Improvement teams should include staff at the working level so that they become involved in the quality improvement effort.

Empowerment means delegating control to the working level. This needs to be done gradually, as people get used to the idea and as they acquire the skills. Training is needed to provide staff with the skills to control their production processes, and to investigate and solve problems.

2.2.3. Quality Measurement Systems

Measuring quality costs is important. There is an old adage that if you can't measure it you can't manage it. Measures of quality costs provide the information needed to analyse where the excess costs are occurring. You can then target improvement projects to reduce them.

If all of your needs are satisfied you judge that you have received quality. Quality is more than meeting a product specification because a specification only provides a minimum set of requirements. Quality is being delighted that your expectations have been met and exceeded. Companies need to develop a range of measures that get a handle on various categories of quality costs. These include quality costs that show up in the factory and quality costs that show up when the product has reached the customer.

Quality costs include the costs of scrapping material during production, the cost of reworking defective material, the cost of repairing products, and warranty costs. Typically businesses rely on inspection to weed out defects and when defects are found products are either scrapped or reworked. This is rather like having two factories under one roof.

There is one factory turning out good quality products that comply with customer requirements. Then there is another hidden factory which turns out defective products for the scrap metal merchants and rework products that were defective in the first place. This hidden factory is maybe half or a quarter the size of the real factory.

Quality cost are enormous and they must be measured if there is to be any hope of improvement. The information provided by a well designed cost tracking system enables management to focus their efforts on the high cost areas and to track how well the improvement efforts are going. Quality costs can be broken down into failure costs, appraisal costs and preventive costs. Failure costs usually account for the major proportion of quality costs in companies that do not have an effective quality programme. They include costs associated with scrap, rework, repair and warranty actions.

Appraisal costs are associated with inspection and testing activities to sort out good products from the bad. Prevention costs are the costs of the quality management programme, for instance design reviews, failure analysis, quality function deployment matrix and quality training. Prevention costs are typically quite low. When Quality Management is introduced one would expect prevention costs to increase and failure costs and appraisal costs to go down.

Quality measurement should begin with a system for documenting non conformances. Every time an item fails a test, a purchased item is rejected, a statistically controlled process exceeds its limits, a product is returned from a customer, the non conformance must be documented. A computerised data base should be used to enter and store this information because the volume of data is too great for a manual system to be effective.

The information should be recorded in a way that allows easy analysis. The idea is not to produce piles of paper but to collect data that can be analysed to provide direction to the quality improvement programme. A computer is necessary because one needs to be able to sort failure costs into categories, for instance by product type, supplier, or type of failure. There are many off the shelf network database programmes that can be used. The information should be displayed using graphs which show trends, bar charts and pie charts that indicate rankings.

2.2.4. Problem Solution

Problem solving consists of identifying the root causes of a problem and implementing actions to correct the situation. There is a simple four step approach to problem solving which can be applied to many situations:

1. The first step is to define the problem

2. The next step is to seek the root causes of the problem. There is a tendency to jump to the first cause that comes to mind. This is hazardous as it can focus on the wrong cause or simply correct a symptom. In many situations the root cause can be found by brainstorming. More complex problems require more sophisticated techniques, such as cause/effect diagrams or system failure analysis.

3. Once the likely causes of the problem have been found one should identify a variety of potential solutions and select the best to implement.

There is a ranking order for selecting solutions:

1. The best solutions is one that eliminates the problem altogether, making the system foolproof

2. In some cases the problem cannot be eliminated so one may relax the requirements

3. When these solutions are not feasible the problem may be resolved by training personnel to control the circumstances that contribute to the problem

4. A least preferred solutions is to resort to inspection and testing to sort good products from bad

5. The worst solution is to use cautions or warnings of possible hazards

The final step in the problem solving sequence is to evaluate the effectiveness of the solution. This is done after it has been implemented to ensure that the solution really does work. It is also a learning experience for the organisation so that people can learn from the successes and pitfalls experienced by others.

2.2.5. Analysis of System Failure

The system failure analysis is a sophisticated approach to

finding the root cause of failures in complex systems. A system may be a production system that is malfunctioning or it may be a product that has failed in service.

The analysis begins by identifying the failure symptoms. The next step is to evaluate the failure causes by using a fault tree analysis technique. This is simply a method of systematically determining all the potential causes of the failure and depicting them graphically. When the fault tree has been compiled it is possible to see how the possible causes relate to each other and how they can contribute to the failure.

The next step is to study each possible failure mode to investigate the likelihood that it may have contributed to the problem. This is done by compiling a failure mode assessment and assignment matrix. Team members are then assigned to investigate each potential cause more closely. There are various techniques that can be used:

1. A 'what's different' analysis identifies the factors that have been changed and may have contributed to the failure.

2. A pedigree analysis examines the documents (including test data, inspection data, supplier material information) related to the components and sub assemblies identified in the fault tree.

3. Hypothetical failure modes can be investigated by making special tests on components to induce failures.

4. Various diagnostic tests can be done on hardware components as the failed equipment is stripped down for inspection.

The beauty of the failure mode analysis is that it offers a systematic method of determining all the possible modes of failure and investigating them to determine the most likely causes.

2.2.6. Teams

Teams are to be used for problem solving. Teams have a number of advantages over individuals. A properly constituted team has a much richer mix of skills to bring to bear on a problem. Most work processes cut across functional boundaries, so a cooperative effort is required to solve process problems. Management needs to have a structured approach to problem solving. While it is important to encourage everyone to suggest areas for improvement, especially at the working level where staff are in a good position to see the problems and the improvement opportunities, one must avoid a scatter gun approach.

The improvement effort must focus on improving the most critical problems. Without control and direction it is possible to have dozens of teams, some studying the same problem and some working on problems that are not important. There must be a high level Steering Team that approves improvement projects, tracks their progress, monitors the results and verifies the benefits. Project team leaders should report to the Steering Team right up to the time of implementation and after an evaluation of the results has been made.

2.2.7. Quality Function Deployment

Quality Function Deployment provides a systematic method for unearthing the customers' needs and expectations, making trade-offs when these needs are in conflict, and ensuring that the needs are effectively incorporated into the final product. When used effectively, this method enables a business to bring a new product to market faster. The product will be more likely to hit the requirements of the target market, making it easier to build market share and stay ahead of the competition.

Quality Function Deployment is a multi-disciplinary tool that requires marketing, design, production and sales to work together to ensure that the needs of the customer are deployed into the product design. The analysis uses a graphic method to portray the information in the form of a matrix. The resulting matrix has a shape that looks like a house with a peaked roof. For this reason it is sometimes called the 'house of quality'.

While it provides a method for showing where trade-offs must be made, it does not take away the need for exercising technical and commercial judgement to make the trade-offs.

2.2.8. Inventory Management

The Economic Ordering Quantity is the term used to describe the ideal amount and frequency of inventory ordering. Inventories carry huge costs. The warehouse to store the inventory costs money, inventory costs money, stocks of partly finished goods along the production line costs money, and the amount of money to pay for these is increased by way of interest charges. Inventory costs are considered a necessary evil to provide a cushion against unforseen demands.

The two critical factors that need to be improved for Just-in-Time inventory control to work are set up time and defect rates. When one can change the set up on machines quickly it is possible to manufacture precise quantities on demand. Defect rates are important too. If the products have no defects one can manufacture the exact quantities with no need for a cushion.

2.2.9. Value Improvement

Value improvement differs from cost reduction. Cost reduction usually results in cheapening the product.

Value improvement is aimed at cutting costs while at the same time continuing to surpass customer expectations. It requires that one analyse the cost structure of the product, relate this to the customer requirements, and eliminate or reduce those costs that are unnecessary. There are two approaches to value improvement.

The first is a simple one which is aimed at eliminating all the costs which are obviously unnecessary. The second is to make a systematic analysis of the entire cost structure with the objective of identifying and reducing those cost drivers that are not necessary. The first step is to go after the easy and the obvious. Quite frequently the cost elements are easy to spot if one makes the effort to get the employees involved.

The second way is to make a systematic onslaught on costs. This is more difficult. Difficult or not, it must be done. It is necessary to identify the cost structure of the product. Costs can be analysed on a component by component basis, or one can analyse the organisational contribution to the cost structure. If the information is presented in the form of a pie chart it is easy to see where the main costs occur. When the cost structure has been identified, the next step is to analyse the high cost items, and to use a Quality Functional Deployment analysis to balance costs against customer requirements and whittle away at needless costs.

Costs can be cut and quality enhanced by setting up Continuous Improvement teams to improve the internal manufacturing processes. One should also work with suppliers to reduce the costs of purchased items. These frequently make up a large proportion of the total costs.

2.2.10. Supplier Teaming

For many products the purchased items make up a large portion of their cost structure. It follows that suppliers must be brought into the quality improvement effort. Communications are important. Explaining that one expects all the requirements to be met is a good start. Make sure that the supplier does not get sloppy and use the receiving inspection function in lieu of their own inspection. When problems arise with quality or delivery call the supplier to let them know the problem. Suppliers should be involved in quality improvement teams and in many cases they should be consulted during the development of a new product.

Frequently suppliers can offer valuable insights into the product development stage, suggest what will and what will not work. They can bring the benefit of their experience with other customers. When making purchase decisions one should focus on the overall cost of the product being purchased not on the initial price. The total cost of doing business includes the cost of handling defects, the cost of late deliveries and the cost of changing from one supplier to another. Low cost is not the same as low price.

One should cut down on the number of suppliers and adopt a policy of dealing with fewer, better suppliers. By only dealing with the best suppliers it is possible to build a beneficial relationship which should lead to working together to improve the quality and delivery of incoming products. The long term objective should be to develop a relationship with a supplier based on trust. It should lead to co-operation on quality improvement projects which drives down costs and improves quality and delivery.

3

BENCHMARKING EFFECTIVELY

Benchmarking is the process of identifying, understanding, and adapting outstanding practices from organisations anywhere in the world to help your organisation improve its performance. It is a highly respected practice in the business world. It is an activity that looks outward to find best practice and high performance and then measures actual business operations against those goals.

The following are some guidelines when looking at benchmarking for your industry:

1. It is usually appropriate to benchmark companies that are similar in size and function. For instance, if you are a small company it would not be very useful to compare yourself to Microsoft. In many industries different size, volume and sales can have totally different sets of benchmarks.

2. Try to use several standards if possible. By comparing standards you can get a more realistic view of how you are doing.

3. Try to get the most current standards possible. Benchmarks several years old have little value — you are seeing what everyone used to do.

4. Look for standards in trade publications/ organisations and also in publications.

5. Remember benchmark figures are often averages and may not be representative of the best in your industry.

6. Remember that current measures are history. In today's rapidly changing business environment those figures may be changing.

7. Compare the benchmarks to your financial reports. Make this a part of your financial report review. Be sure to share relevant information with managers and staff.

8. Before you begin the benchmarking process, determine what objectives and benefits you would like to obtain. Also determine what measures you will apply.

9. If you are sincere about improvements compare your business to the top businesses in your industry. Simply knowing there are minimal businesses in your industry provides little value.

10. Look outside your industry to get an idea of how similar businesses are doing. You may find that other industries do things differently and get better results.

11. Put your benchmarking findings into the context of your business' development, especially if you are growing quickly.

12. Don't forget that the idea of benchmarking is to get improvement. Simply knowing the figures and ratios will not get results. Action gets results.

Those businesses that use benchmarking effectively understand that profitability and growth come from a clear picture of how the business is doing. This is more than comparing figures to past company performance. By identifying what the better companies are doing you can get a sense of what you need to do.

3.1. BENCHMARKING PROCESS

Benchmarking is a deliberate, time consuming process requiring organisational discipline, and a strong and active commitment from senior management. The desire to close any performance gap requires tough operational, organisational and resource allocation choices, which must be supported by upper management, and backed by a willingness to adapt and learn from others". Leading practitioners have formalised the benchmarking process into five general phases:

3.1.1. Planning

It is important to have an understanding of your organisation's existing internal processes, products, and services before commencing a benchmarking study. A thorough knowledge and understanding of the internal environment is critical for several reasons:

1. It positions the organisation to readily determine the potential gaps between its outcomes or activities and those of best practices organisations,

2. It may reveal important sources of information and assistance as well as benchmarking opportunities,

3. It facilitates the selection of appropriate benchmarking partners and meaningful performance indicators, and

4. The exchange of information is the cornerstone of benchmarking.

Without an internal review, an organisation may not be able to engage in the meaningful exchange of information and, as a result, may encounter difficulties in obtaining information from others.

Identify the internal clients of benchmarking, their requirements, the outputs of the benchmarking effort and gain the endorsement of management benchmarking, their requirements, the outputs of the benchmarking effort and gain the endorsement of management:

Managers of individual processes are typically focused on those processes that affect their operation. A clear understanding of what use will be made of benchmarking information is critical to the success of the project. An organisation will need to set parameters around the resources established for the benchmarking project such as the available time, money and personnel devoted to the task. At this stage, it is also useful to consider how benchmarking results will be used as this may indicate what should be benchmarked and the level of detail required.

Gaining the support and "buy-in" of senior management is crucial at this point. While senior management commitment is critical to ensuring that the project results are implemented, the day-to-day efforts associated with the benchmarking initiative will need to be driven by the managers of the financial functions to be benchmarked.

Establish the benchmarking or process improvement team benchmarking or process improvement team: Forming a project team with the knowledge and capacity for planning, communicating the results and implementing the findings is critical for setting a clear and concise direction for the project. This also includes setting limits on the number of benchmarking team members and estimating the number of processes to be benchmarked. "The team should be made up of individuals who are most knowledgeable about internal operations, are more likely to be affected by the changes due to benchmarking, and who are flexible and open to change.

Benchmarking involves changes to processes and ways of doing business which may be met with scepticism and resistance on the part of staff. There are always choices about how to move through the change process. Sometimes it makes sense to move quickly; whereas at other times it is preferable to invest time in crafting the change process carefully to minimise disruption and cost. To be effective and increase the likelihood of success of the financial management benchmarking exercise, the benchmarking team needs to formulate a change management plan and update this plan periodically. The key components of this plan should include:

1. Clear articulation of benchmarking objectives and their linkage to the overall departmental as well as finance organisation vision,

2. Strong and visible senior management commitment throughout the process,

3. Identification of a critical mass of people from all levels of the finance organisation who will push for the change and demonstrate ownership and commitment,

4. Honest, open and regular communications with staff, and

5. A clear migration approach from the current to the future state based on benchmarking results.

Although included as part of the planning phase, change management is an activity that would need to occur throughout the benchmarking process.

3.1.2. Data Gathering

The following provide some general guidelines for data gathering.

3.1.2.1. Questionnaire

"A questionnaire is the foundation for any good benchmarking study and provides a common communication link among the benchmarking participants. Prepared before initial contact, it ensures that the team has a good understanding of the processes being benchmarked, and is verified by those who do the actual work".

3.1.2.2. Surveys

When conducting a mail or telephone survey, the appropriate target population is identified and asked to respond to a questionnaire. It is sometimes necessary to offer some incentives to ensure a rate of response that will provide reliable results.

3.1.2.3. Personal visit and interview

"The initial contact should be made by the benchmarking team leader or by senior management, especially where sensitive data is to be considered. The data analysis methodology should be carefully considered to ensure that the data is in a format conducive to analysis". A two-member team is considered ideal for a visit: one to ask the questions, another to take notes and observe the interview process.

3.1.3. Analysis and Integration

Analysis of data is a precursor for the identification of performance gaps and the underlying causes of such gaps. The validity of benchmark data is affected by the degree of comparability between organisations. In some instances, such as where one organisation is heavily automated while another is not, performance measures may not be readily comparable. In these cases, the benchmarking team would need to normalise the data in order to draw accurate conclusions. Data is normalised on a ratio basis using factors such as:

1. Size (budget dollars/employee),

2. Age (infrastructure, IT systems), and

3. Working environment (fiscal pressures, regulatory requirements).

A basic tool for analysing performance gaps is a matrix chart listing performance measures for each of the benchmarking partners. This matrix format has been found to be useful in highlighting performance gaps. In evaluating performance gaps, the focus of the benchmarking team should be future oriented. Instead of targeting current levels of performance, the team should look beyond today's performance levels and targets to understand the level of performance that will be required in the future and the enablers required to achieve that level. A prospective approach is essential for achieving and maintaining superior performance.

The analysis of data should be related to the original purpose of the study. If the purpose of the study is to gather qualitative business practices and methods, organisations will need to synthesise the raw data using any of the following tools:

1. Charts,

2. Graphs, and

3. Descriptive anecdotes.

The analysis of data should lead to the determination of benchmark performance and to the understanding of the practices used to achieve them. The performance gap represents the difference between the internal performance and that of the best in the field, and could be either negative, zero or positive.

Where performance gaps exist, the next step would consist of designing and implementing a performance improvement plan and, subsequently, recalibrating the benchmarks.

3.1.4. Implementation and Execution

At this stage, the benchmarking team presents management with its findings to obtain acceptance of the analysis, conclusions and implementation actions necessary to close the performance gap. The presentation to management should include the goals or planned performance to narrow, close or exceed the benchmark standard, based on the organisation's objectives. The successful implementation of a performance improvement plan requires senior management sponsorship and buy-in.

Performance improvement plans may range from incremental improvement to the redesign of processes to reengineering. A business case outlining the cost/benefit of the chosen level of improvement is often necessary to secure senior management commitment. "Once management acceptance is obtained, the organisation should develop a set of action plans to achieve the new goals. It is critical that actions be well defined to ensure their successful implementation. For each action, a description of time frame, responsibility, resources requirements and its impact on the performance gap should be included. Action plans should also be reviewed with the staff in affected areas to obtain their commitment. After the implementation stage begins, progress should be monitored against milestones established in the action plans".

3.2. BENCHMARKING BENEFITS

Benchmarking is a tool that provides goals for realistic

improvement and helps you understand the changes required for improving performance.

Provide meaningful performance information: "All levels of government need reliable ways of assessing the relative performance of public programmes in order to be able to set overall priorities and strategies. Benchmarking can assist public sector managers improve the quality of their performance information. Such improvements can, in turn, help organisations better meet external and internal accountability requirements. Benchmarking information often adds an important comparative perspective to organisational outputs.

Improve strategic planning and provide an assessment of the organisation's strengths and weaknesses: The organisation can learn how to plan for the long term more effectively by seeing how other organisations have reached better levels of performance through their own strategic planning. Benchmarking allows management to determine where major problems lie, and what can be done to strengthen weak areas. Areas of excellence will also surface, enabling the organisation to continue with what it is doing well.

Establish challenging performance goals and stimulate better performance: "Benchmarking is all about comparison, and comparison can be a driving force to spur on organisational or individual performance". Realising what an organisation is doing wrong, or could do better, leads to easier planning for future target performance levels. Management will know where it stands in terms of performance and what has to be done to get where it wants to be. This should result in more realistic goals being set.

Benchmarking of activities or functions can help senior managers and staff determine how organisations and programmes are performing in relation to the leading organisations in their field. The technique can uncover new and creative ideas to assist in performance improvement. Benchmarking serves as a tool, among others, to assist managers in their mandate to modernise and improve financial management in the federal government.

Foster implementation of best practices and lead to significant savings: Benchmarking and other comparative information can be used to address pressures by identifying ways to streamline processes, or opportunities to improve the allocation of resources. The implementation of best practices found in other organisations through benchmarking will help the organisation become more efficient and effective.

4

MANAGING TOTAL QUALITY

In almost every category of products and services, today's competitive market is characterised by accelerating changes, innovation, and massive amounts of new information. Much of this rapid evolution in markets is fuelled by changing customer needs. Significant customer behaviour and market changes happen almost overnight. Changes in market preference or technology, which used to take years, may now take place in a few short months.

Commitment to quality and customer satisfaction programmes are essential for a small business to compete against both smaller and larger competitors. Think about "post-sale" customer satisfaction (or managing customer "dissatisfaction") programmes as a way to reinforce customers' buying preferences for your products and services for their current and future purchases. A new company or a small business has limited financial, personnel, and capital plant/equipment resources and is especially vulnerable to instability brought on by rapid changes in customer behaviour.

One way to help ensure your business success is to make quality and customer satisfaction the number one priority for all employees in your company. Make sure your company is providing "customer management," not just "product management." Larger companies committed to TQM programmes may appoint a special manager or VP of quality. In smaller companies, this task is usually undertaken by the chief executive officer (CEO) or the owner. There are many aspects of successful TQM programme implementation. And it may require months or years to fully incorporate TQM into every employee's value system. There are several keys to a successful TQM programme for small businesses:

4.1. COMMITMENT TO QUALITY

Quality work and customer satisfaction must be a commitment of all employees. A small company has great potential advantage over larger companies in implementing a TQM programme with employees. There are fewer people to communicate with, and the manager in charge of implementing the TQM programme is generally the owner or CEO. The CEO can make timely, binding decisions about TQM programmes.

Personnel in all jobs must understand and commit to the TQM programme and work as a team. Company personnel must have permission to go beyond the normal barriers between functional jobs to communicate in a timely manner on behalf of providing quality and customer satisfaction. All employees, regardless of job, status, or tenure, must understand and commit to customer satisfaction as a number one priority. Small or large companies serious about making the commitment to TQM and customer satisfaction must:

1. Provide specific programmes, written guidelines, and training sessions for all company personnel.

2. Allow for decision-making and mistakes by all company personnel.

3. Provide a specific timetable for training, behavioural modification, and feedback.

4. Follow up with customers to obtain feedback on the success of the new TQM programmes.

5. Commit to weeding out uncooperative company personnel.

Top management must not only commit to TQM and set daily examples, they must also give explicit permission to employees to act in the same manner. People may also need training and written guidelines to fully empower them. This also reduces the personal risks of adapting new behavior within the company and toward customers.

Some company employees who do not have regular direct contact with customers (e.g., shipping and receiving, plant workers, financial analysts, etc.) may be confused about what their new role would be with a TQM/customer satisfaction programme. The answer is the more everyone in your company knows about your customer's business, needs, complaints, and sources of satisfaction with your company, the more motivated, productive, and efficient they will be. Day-to-day activities of an internal staff employee, who has never even spoken or met with your customers, also affects the quality of your company's products and services. And ultimately, all company employees affect customer value and satisfaction.

Therefore, owners or managers in a small company must commit to sharing and communicating customer information and customer feedback with all their company personnel. This information should consist of the customer's business description, personality, expectations, problems, opportunities, and periodic survey feedback. Managers must also allow employees to share and discuss this same customer information, where confidentiality is not essential, to encourage fellow employees to improve quality and customer satisfaction.

4.2. IMPROVING QUALITY AND SATISFACTION

Improving quality and customer satisfaction must also be a commitment of all employees. The more participation by company employees in quality programmes and the more ways they think up to improve customer satisfaction, the better the quality! Once your people understand and accept new TQM programmes, regular discussion sessions should be scheduled to discuss quality problems and opportunities at least once each month.

To the degree possible, company personnel should be directly involved with the creation, modification, and writing of evolving quality guidelines and suggestions for improvement. Involvement may range from the simple suggestion box to written plan suggestions with preliminary cost savings/business increase analysis. It's important that people in different functions or departments are encouraged to talk with and get help from each other.

Once company TQM programme training is underway, careful attention to each person's commitment level and TQM actions is necessary. If problems occur with some individuals resisting or actively sabotaging adoption of TQM, written documentation is recommended for each meeting and counselling session with the problem employee. If the problem is not resolved in a suitable period of time, a decision will have to be made on the future tenure of the problem employee. There is no place to hide a problem employee in a company committed to quality and customer satisfaction.

4.3. INCORPORATING TQM IN ALL ACTIVITIES

Every company activity must incorporate quality and customer satisfaction, including all communications with customers and suppliers. If a single team member is not doing his or her best, the performance of the entire team is negatively affected. Quality and customer satisfaction is everyone's job. Small companies are often sales-driven, instead of market-driven or customer-driven. Strong sales talent is the most common way a small company grows. So it is natural for a sales-driven company to think about TQM improvements in terms of "where it counts the most," in sales.

But the sales force cannot succeed without good quality products and services that are distinct from and valued by customers when compared to what competitors provide. Sales also needs good support from manufacturing and shipping in terms of correctly filling the order, on time, every time. Sales may need quality technical support to help obtain the sale and to service the customer after the sale. Small companies are often too busy trying to find and close new customers. They may not think about or have the time to follow up on current customers to see if they are indeed satisfied.

How can small businesses incorporate quality and concern for customer satisfaction into every company function? Often, even critical tasks, like monthly closings for company P&Ls (profit and loss statements), get delayed because there are not enough hours or people to do everything. Some solutions are given below:

1. Total company commitment begins at the top. The head of the company must commit to total quality marketing and customer satisfaction, live it every day, and institute procedures and information systems to ensure all employees do the same.

2. Customer service, customer satisfaction, and customer commitment become the top company priorities. The entire company must work to support the sales staff and customers. For example,

Nordstrom Department store personnel will never be criticised for doing too much for customers. They will be criticised for doing too little!

3. Employee hiring and training programmes for quality work and customer orientation need to be implemented and enforced. For example, Nordstrom want ads seek employees who are "people-oriented" and who find satisfaction in going out of their way to help others. Regular training programmes, with weekly department meetings to discuss customer problems, solutions, and complaints and next step actions for customers, are necessary.

4. Customer feedback on performance must be sought and received on a regular basis. It is not enough for a small business to be satisfied that it is doing a better job with its customers than the competition. The customers must also think so and provide at least quarterly feedback on company supplier performance.

5. Suppliers committed to quality must be sought out, so that customer satisfaction is a priority all the way up and down the chain of distribution.

Quill Corporation has a one-page "Customer Bill of Rights" that was created in the early days of the company by the founders. Every company employee must read and commit to providing these "customer rights." Quill is as well-known for its customer service as its extensive office products, competitive prices, and frequent promotions.

Employee feedback on customer satisfaction. A short one-page or half-page form can be used by all employees to note customer satisfaction events or problems that need to be addressed, as they happen each day. This form should be circulated to all appropriate departments within one week. Circulation of the form within one day may be possible for small companies. A summary of these internal company department comments on improving customer satisfaction (or solving customer problems) should be circulated each week to all employees to inform, educate, and improve total company problem-solving for customers.

Feedback from customers. Do you have a regular feedback method to confirm when your company is doing its job well with customers, or to detect problems when it is not? How timely is the feedback? Is it actionable? Once customers know that you are interested in feedback, your company must act on what they say and then provide status reports or presentations on the successful disposition of each problem or opportunity. Consider staging a quarterly review with your key customers to provide:

1. A summary of sales information for year-to-date and previous years, along with an analysis of the business.

2. A summary of current customer service problems and how they were addressed by your company.

3. A summary of customer service improvements.

4. A forum for candid customer feedback, with a short, one-page form.

Consider staging a quarterly review with your key customers to provide:

1. A summary of sales information for year-to-date and previous years, along with an analysis of the business.

2. A summary of current customer service problems and how they were addressed by your company.

3. A summary of customer service improvements.

4. A forum for candid customer feedback, with a short, one-page form.

4.4. TQM AND SUPPLIERS

You can maintain and deliver the quality of your products and services only if all personnel and all companies involved in your chain of suppliers are quality-oriented and customer-oriented. By definition, superior quality and customer satisfaction compared to your competition depend upon the exceptional. You and your suppliers will have to go above and beyond normal procedures, delivery dates, lead times, and other standards to maintain quality and provide superior customer satisfaction. This may be required occasionally, or all the time, depending upon the customer and type of industry and business.

Only suppliers committed to the same attitudes about quality and customer satisfaction will be able to support you and your company under exceptional circumstances and demands by customers. Companies committed to quality and customer satisfaction have the dual responsibility of seeking suppliers who are like-minded and maintaining their commitment.

4.5. Costs of TQM

It doesn't have to cost more to make quality and customer satisfaction your priority. The idea of "quality" is free. Studies on successful implementation of TQM programmes and customer service show a significant improvement in company efficiencies, sales, and profitability, often with fewer people and at less cost than before. Most companies, small and large, operate well below 100 percent of their potential efficiency.

What is your evaluation of operating efficiency for your company? 50 percent? 75 percent? 40 percent? Some of this underutilised potential may be measured in quantitative terms, such as plant capacities, the ratio of parts meeting standard to the number of rejects, or the turnaround time for orders to delivery. However, much of this underutilised potential is more subtle, difficult to see, and difficult to correct. What is the cost-savings for increased good will or customer loyalty? These intangibles can lower costs and yield tangible gains in productivity, sales, and ultimately profits.

When each employee is personally committed to quality and customer satisfaction, people will be doing more things right and better the first time. This results in lower costs, less waste, and higher productivity. Much of the success of Japan's auto industry in the 70s, 80s, and today rests *less* on innovation and more on a commitment to quality and efficiency.

4.6. TQM: DEMANDS OF SIGNIFICANT CHANGES

Continuous quality improvement is the hallmark of successful companies, worldwide. Many successful companies have adopted continuous quality improvement as the number one operational principle for all employees and departments. Continuous quality improvement does not always mean a limited quality improvement. Entire new product categories can be created by exploiting anomalies in quality and customer satisfaction. A key insight into the need for significant change in quality or customer service is to examine:

1. The history of the company: how it first became successful.

2. The history of the category: how it grew or changed.

3. The history of competitors: how they grew or changed.

4. The behavioural needs of customers: have they evolved.

What factors made your company successful? Does your company still have this edge? For example, many small companies are successful because they specialise in a small-volume category segment that a larger company could not make money on or would not commit resources to. A small company may focus on a narrow segment of specialised customers. For example, think about a machine shop that produces only high-tech machinery for analysing exotic metals for the aerospace industry. There may not be enough business for more that one or two such supplier companies in the country. Being sensitive to changing customer needs, wants, and evolving technology or service requirements is critical for such a small company to survive.

The rapid pace of information systems and technological advances may not only create new competitors, it may provide substitutes for your category's products and services that did not exist a few years ago. For example, it is becoming more common for fast food providers to compete head-to-head with local "standard restaurants" in business areas via fax orders. In the past, fast food restaurants did not consider regular restaurants as direct competitors because of their larger and slower menu preparation.

However, standard restaurants now advertise directly to businesses for "fax-ahead menu" selection, so that customers' meals can be ready within minutes of arrival, exactly like a fast-food place. If your company has lost its niche, is less distinctive in its products and services, or is contemplating starting a new business, significant improvements in quality and customer service or satisfaction may be required to survive. At the same time, do not overlook the possibility of small improvements in company functions.

Small advantages in all company functions can set your quality and customer satisfaction apart from the competition. For many small companies, the secret of continued business success in competing against larger companies is to do everything a little bit better than the competition. Many companies search only for the great quantum leap in quality or products that will provide a competitive edge, often at the expense of making smaller improvements. But those quantum leaps may be few and far between, while the chance to make small improvements is there almost every day.

Quality (and uniqueness) of product is important. But it is also important to have quality in serving customers, quality in advertising and promotion programmes, quality in packaging, in company trade show booths, in design, engineering, written and oral communications, trade logos or symbols, and so on.

Sometimes, a small company has an advantage in simply delivering products and services as ordered by customers, on time, every time. Many local distribution companies have trouble satisfying orders, meeting delivery turnaround times, and keeping out-of-stocks down for their grocery store and mass outlet customers. The number of items stocked by modern chain stores and therefore direct-store-delivery distributors has multiplied several fold in the last decade, going from less than 5,000 to close to 20,000 items per average store.

Distributors struggle to fulfil "just the basics" of routine delivery of ordered items on a daily basis. The distribution complexity, evolving store item counts, and growing end user customer needs and wants for variety and "mass customisation" is rapidly changing the way new and current products will be delivered to stores and customers in the future. The giant retail stores of today are rapidly approaching a physical limitation on their ability to receive and stock products in their stores on a daily basis.

Try a quality improvement exercise: Every company, regardless of size, can improve quality and customer service. A simple exercise to improve quality is to track an order from its inception to final delivery. Try this checklist and see if any improvements can be made:

1. How are products and services sold (with what materials)?

2. How and by whom is the order obtained from your customer?

3. How is the order recorded for your company and your customer?

4. How is the order processed within your company?

5. Is there a system to check for any order discounts to customers?

6. How long does it take to process and deliver the order to the customer?

7. Do you have any accuracy checks for the order, with the customer and internally?

8. How is the final product or service delivered to your customer?

9. Have you checked customer relationship "manners" with everyone who has direct contact with your customers?

10. Have you allowed everyone associated with order processing to meet periodically and discuss improvement possibilities?

11. Do you have a customer follow up procedure for orders?

12. Do you review your order and service satisfaction level at least quarterly with each customer?

5

HOW TO CARRY OUT A CONTINUOUS PROCESS IMPROVEMENT

Quality is a never ending quest and Continuous Process Improvement (CPI) is a never ending effort to discover and eliminate the main causes of problems. It accomplishes this by using small-steps improvements, rather than implementing one huge improvement. CPI means making things better. It is not fighting fires. Its goal is not to blame people for problems or failures. It is simply a way of looking at how we can do our work better. When we take a problem solving approach, we often never get to the root causes because our main goal is to put out the fire. But when we engage in process improvement, we seek to learn what causes things to happen and then use this knowledge to:

1. Reduce variation.

2. Remove activities that have no value to the organisation.

3. Improve customer satisfaction.

Process improvement is important as it has often been said that process account for 80% of all problems while people account for the remaining 20%.

One way to get CPI started is to set up a Steering Committee (SC). Although everyone in the organisation is responsible for CPI, the SC follows all ideas from conception to completion. Some organisations might have several SCs working on different processes, departments, or systems; while smaller organisations might set up one SC to oversee all CPI projects.

Normally, there is one SC that oversees all CPI projects within a physical area. It in turn, passes each CPI suggestion on to a CPI team that carries that project out to completion. At the very least, the SC must contain members who can approve a project

CPI has been described using a number of models. This chapter will use the system approach or ADDIE (Analysis, Design, Development, Implement, Evaluate) model. There are five phases in this model:

1. *Analysis Phase*: Identify areas of opportunity and target specific problems. These areas and problems are based on team brainstorming sessions, process definition sessions, recommendations forwarded to the team by organisational members, and other various analysis techniques.

2. *Design Phase*: Generate solutions through brainstorming sessions. Identify the required resources to implement the chosen solution and identify baselines to measure.

3. *Development Phase*: Formulate a detailed procedure for implementing the approved solution.

4. *Implementation Phase*: Execute the solution.

5. *Evaluation Phase*: Build measurement tools, monitor implementation, and evaluate measurements to baseline. This phase is performed throughout the entire process.

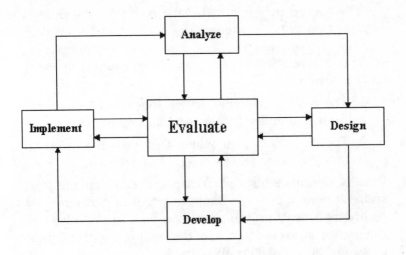

Figure 1. Dynamic model of continuous process Improvement

5.1. PROCESS DEFINITION

Building a task and event relationship is called Process Definition. A process is a planned series of actions that advances a material or procedure from one stage of completion to the next. It includes the steps and decisions involved in the way work is accomplished.

The first step of process definition is to identify the boundaries. This is where the process begins and ends. The beginning of a process starts with a trigger that causes a specific action to be taken by a person, another process, or work group. The ending occurs when the results get passed on to another person, process, or work group. The beginning trigger starts when someone performs an action on an input that they receive from a supplier. The input can be physical, such as raw material, parts, a person to be interviewed, etc.; or information, such as a computer printout, request form, etc.

The ending trigger is when the results of the process is passed on to the customer. The output can be physical, such as a television set, new hire, etc.; or information, such as a typed letter, grant, etc. Every person at every level has two roles:

1. The role of customer where they receive a trigger from a supplier (either external or internal).
2. The role of supplier where they pass the result on to a customer (either external or internal).

Process Definition lists what happens between the start and end points. It includes all the activities performed by each department, group, or person who are involved in the process. Activities are the major "works" that transform an input into an output.

5.2. OBJECTIVES OF PROCESS PERFORMANCE

Process Performance Objectives are brief and concise plans that contain an action statement. They include:

1. *Direction* - e.g. reduce, increase
2. *Measurement* - e.g. hours, cycle time
3. *Process* - e.g. receive shipments, build widget
4. *Solution* - e.g. by implementing, changing
5. *Target* - a number or goal to aim for (targets should always be reviewed with the organisation's leadership to see if they concur with their goals)

Number of people or resources involved in a process

5.3. WAYS TO CARRY OUT A CONTINUOUS IMPROVEMENT PROJECT

There are many ways to carry out a Continuous Improvement project. A generic approach is described here which should suit most situations. No projects are the same and so the approach should be tailored to fit the job. These are the main steps as given below:

5.3.1. Set up the Project Team

The Steering Team will have defined the terms of reference, selected the team leader and given some general direction about the composition of the Project Team. A team is more effective than an individual for problem solving because it can draw on a wider range of experience and skills. There are two types of skills required - technical and problem solving skills. Team members must be chosen to ensure that someone on the team is knowledgeable in every aspect of the process being studied. Major stockholders and customers should be represented.

A low level process team should have people from the working level because they have a better understanding of how a process actually works. A high level process team should include managers because they have a broader perspective. The team members must be knowledgeable in team building skills and understand the tools and strategies that can be used for problem solving. It is likely that time will have to be set aside at the first few meetings to provide training. The downloadable file on Team Effectiveness describes the factors to be considered in building effective teams.

5.3.2. Define the Scope

The Project Team should review the scope of the project and negotiate changes with the Steering Team. The team leader should talk to the customer and end user to find out what they think the problems are and define their expectations. The scope of the project include the statement of the problem, a definition of the boundaries, the magnitude of improvement goals, a target date for completion and the resources available.

5.3.3. Set the Goals

One of the fundamental approaches of Continuous Improvement is to look at the process from the customer's point of view. The starting point should be to find out what the customer and the end user want. The end user may not be the customer. They may be downstream from the process or they may be external. Whoever the customer or end user is, the goal should be to find out their expectations and meet them.

Firstly, the team should talk to the customer and find out how they use the product or service, what problems they have with it, and how it can be enhanced. The information obtained from these interviews should be analysed to determine which aspects of the product or service should be improved and the extent to which the product or service meets the needs of the customer.

Based on this analysis the team should define the project goals. These goals will likely differ from the original goals set by the Steering Team. It is the job of the Team Leader to go back to the Steering Team and negotiate any changes. The new set of goals are likely to be more realistic and useful than the original goals set by the Steering Team. The team should develop a very clear understanding of what is expected from the project. The goals should be quantified and used as a benchmark to measure the success.

5.3.4. Understand the Process

The next step is to understand how the process presently works. Before the Project Team can attempt to improve the process it must understand how it works now and what it is supposed to do. There are two approaches to understanding the present process. One is descriptive, the other is graphic:

Process Description: A good way to understand the process is to describe it. One benefit of describing the process is that it sometimes leads to the discovery of obvious problems and solutions that can be fixed quickly.

Flow Charts: A flow chart of the process is particularly helpful in obtaining an understanding of how the process works. It provides a visual picture. There are two types of flow charts that are particularly useful. The first is a top down flow chart and the second is a deployment matrix flow chart.

A Top down flow chart shows only the essential steps in a process without detail. Because it focuses on the steps which provide real value, it is particularly useful in helping the team to focus their minds on those steps that must be performed in the final 'improved' process. A Top down flow chart is constructed by first listing the main steps across the top of the page, and then the subsidiary steps are listed, top down, below the main steps. The details are not recorded, for instance rework, inspection, or typing are omitted.

The flow chart provides a picture of the process that the team can use to work on and simplify. It allows people to focus on what should happen instead of what does happen. Usually, most process has evolved in an adhoc manner. When problems have occurred the process has been fixed. The end result is that a simple process has evolved into something complex. A flow chart is a first step to simplify things.

A second type of flow chart is the deployment matrix chart. This is useful because it shows who is responsible for each activity, how they fit into the flow of work and how they relate to others in accomplishing the overall job.

To construct a Deployment Matrix Flow Chart you list the major steps in the process vertically down the left hand side of the page and you list the people or work groups across the top.

5.3.5. Plan the Project

There is no 'right' way to tackle a project. There are many ways and some will work better than others. The basic plan of action will be to:

1. Identify root causes,
2. Develop solutions,
3. Implement the changes,
4. Review the results.

5.3.6. Determine Information Needs

Based on the project goals the team should review what information is needed to analyse the problem. For each goal the team should determine what information is needed to understand how well the process is working. They need to know what information is available and what is not available, and how to collect the information that is not presently available.

5.3.7. Identify the Root Causes

Use brainstorming, cause and effect diagrams or the structure tree to develop a list of possible causes. Begin by defining the problem, then generate ideas as to the cause. When the team has figured out what it thinks the root causes are it should verify the conclusions with data. The team should think about why it is collecting data and what data it needs to verify the conclusions. It is easy to draw the wrong conclusions from erroneous data. Use charts and graphs to analyse the data and have the conclusions checked by others who are knowledgeable in the process. If there are obvious root causes that can be fixed easily then take action to fix them straight away.

5.3.8. Develop Solutions

The ideas for solving the problem should be evaluated against criteria to determine the best solution. The team should define the characteristics of an ideal solution and identify the criteria that must be satisfied and the criteria that are desirable but not absolutely necessary. Constraints to a proposed solution should be identified. A constraint is a factor that limits the selection of a particular solution. These constraints may take the form of budget limits, rules or practices that may make a solution difficult to carry out.

Each possible solution should be evaluated against the criteria for selection. The team should seek to develop a solution which comes closest to solving the root causes, is the easiest to implement, satisfies the criteria for selection, and does not impact on the constraints. There may be occasions where the team identifies constraints which in fact are not real constraints. The team may find some flexibility if it pushes hard enough to have constraints removed.

When the team has selected the best alternative it should obtain feedback from those people who are most affected by the changes. Depending upon the nature of the changes it may be possible to implement them right away. Alternatively it may be necessary to present the recommendations to the Steering Team to obtain approval before they can be implemented.

5.3.9. Implement the Solutions

Define exactly what changes are to be made. Generate a

list of activities that need to be done to accomplish the objective and then figure out the sequence of steps that are required to implement the changes. A schedule of activities should be prepared and milestones defined so that progress can be monitored. Responsibilities for each of the action steps should be defined.

Be sure that all those people who are affected by the changes are properly informed and briefed on the reasons for the changes and that they understand how the changes will take place. It is sometimes better to implement the changes on a pilot basis rather than make a wholesale change across the board.

5.3.10. Review the Results

Monitor the effectiveness of the changes and compare the results of the changes with the original goals of the study. Ask the following questions:

1. Did the team achieve the expected benefits?
2. Where there any unexpected benefits or problems?
3. What can the team learn from these?
4. What can be done to fine tune the solution so that it can be applied on a wider basis?

5.3.11. Standardise the Change

If the improvement project has been successful with one process it should be refined and applied to other processes which are similar. One should not waste time setting up further improvement teams to re-invent the wheel.

6

HOW TO PERFORM IN MY ORGANISATION

Performance management reminds that being busy is not the same as producing results. It reminds us that training, strong commitment and lots of hard work alone are not results. The major contribution of performance management is its focus on achieving results - useful products and services for customers inside and outside the organisation. Performance management redirects our efforts away from business toward effectiveness. Recently, organisations have been faced with challenges like never before.

Increasing competition from businesses across the world has meant that all businesses must be much more careful about the choice of strategies to remain competitive. Everyone in the organisation must be doing what they're supposed to be doing to ensure strategies are implemented effectively. This situation has put more focus on effectiveness, that systems and processes in the organisation be applied in the right way to the right things: to achieve results. All of the results across the organisation must continue to be aligned to achieve the overall results desired by the organisation for it to survive and thrive. Only then it be said that the organisation and its various parts are really performing.

Typically, we think of performance in organisations, we think on the performance of employees. However, performance management should also be focused on:

1. The organisation.

2. Departments (computer support, administration, sales, etc.).

3. Processes (billing, budgeting, product development, financial management, etc.).

4. Programmes (implementing new policies and procedures to ensure a safe workplace; or, for a nonprofit, ongoing delivery of services to a community).

5. Products or services to internal or external customers.

6. Projects (automating the billing process, moving to a new building, etc.).

7. Teams or groups organised to accomplish a result for internal or external customers.

6.1. OVERALL GOAL OF PERFORMANCE MANAGEMENT

The overall goal of performance management is to ensure that the organisation and all of its subsystems (processes, departments, teams, employees, etc.) are working together in an optimum fashion to achieve the results desired by the organisation. Performance management strives to optimise results and alignment of all subsystems to achieve the overall results of the organisation, any focus of performance management within the organisation (whether on department, process, employees, etc.) should ultimately affect overall organisational performance management as well.

Achieving the overall goal requires several ongoing activities, including identification and prioritisation of desired results, establishing means to measure progress toward those results, setting standards for assessing how well results were achieved, tracking and measuring progress toward results, exchanging ongoing feedback among those participants working to achieve results, periodically reviewing progress, reinforcing activities that achieve results and intervening to improve progress where needed.

Performance management brings focus on overall results, measuring results, focused and ongoing feedback about results, and development plans to improve results. The results measurements themselves are not the ultimate priority as much as ongoing feedback and adjustments to meet results. The steps in performance management are also similar to those in a well-designed training process, when the process can be integrated with the overall goals of the organisation. Trainers are focusing much more on results for performance. Many trainers with this priority now call themselves performance consultants.

6.2. STEPS FOR PERFORMANCE MANAGEMENT

The following steps occur in a wide context of many activities geared towards performance improvement in an organisation, for example, activities such as management development, planning, organising and coordinating activities.

1. Review organisational goals to associate preferred organisational results in terms of units of performance, that is, quantity, quality, cost or timeliness (note that the result itself is therefore a measure).

2. Specify desired results for the domain - as guidance, focus on results needed by other domains (e.g., products or services need by internal or external customers).

3. Ensure the domain's desired results directly contribute to the organisation's results.

4. Weight, or prioritise, the domain's desired results.

5. Identify first-level measures to evaluate if and how well the domain's desired results were achieved.

6. Identify more specific measures for each first-level measure if necessary.

7. Identify standards for evaluating how well the desired results were achieved (e.g., "below expectations", "meets expectations" and "exceeds expectations").

8. Document a performance plan - including desired results, measures and standards.

9. Conduct ongoing observations and measurements to track performance.

10. Exchange ongoing feedback about performance.

11. Conduct a performance appraisal (sometimes called performance review).

12. If performance meets the desired performance standard, then reward for performance (the nature of the reward depends on the domain).

13. If performance does not meet the desired performance standards, then develop or update a performance development plan to address the performance gap.

14. Repeat steps 9 to 13 until performance is acceptable, standards are changed, the domain is replaced, management decides to do nothing, etc..

6.3. DEVELOPING A PERFORMANCE PLAN

Most of us are used to thinking of performance management focused on the employee, rather than the organisation, groups, etc. While developing a performance management plan, one should keep the following points in mind:

1. *Review organisational goals to associate preferred organisational results in terms of units of performance, that is, quantity, quality, cost or timeliness*: Organisational goals are often established during strategic planning. Performance management translates these goals to results, which typically are described in terms of quantity, quality, timeliness or cost. Results are the primary products or services desired from the focus of the performance process. Examples are a percentage increase in sales, extent of impact on a certain community, etc. Goals should be "SMART" (an acronym), that is, specific, measurable, acceptable, realistic to achieve and time-bound with a deadline.

   For example, an overall goal may be to increase the organisation's profit by 30% by the end of the next fiscal year. An associated strategy (or sub-goal), among others, may be to increase profit of the Catalogue Department by 50% over the next fiscal year.

2. *Specify desired results for the domain - as guidance, focus on results needed by other domains*: (e.g., to internal or external customers). For example, the operator's results are high-quality, printed images for the internal customer, the Catalogue Department. This aspect of performance management is sometimes called "goal setting", particularly when the focus of the performance process is on employees. Goals should be "SMART" and challenging.

3. *Ensure the domain's desired results directly contribute to the organisation's results*: Aligning results with

organisational results is another unique aspect of performance management process. Do the employee's results directly contribute to the results of the organisation? What organisational goals? How?

4. *Weight, or prioritise, the domain's desired results*: A weight, or prioritisation, is often in the form of percentage-time-spent, or a numeric ranking with "1" as the highest. For example, the employee's results might be weighted as follows:

   — 80% of his time over an 8-hour period, Monday through Friday over the next fiscal year, to be spent running the machine

   — 10% of this time in training

   — 10% of this time in a Quality Circle.

5. *Identify first-level measures to evaluate if and how well the domain's desired results were achieved*: Measures provide information to evaluate accomplishment of results. Measures are usually specified in terms of quantity, quality, timeliness or cost. For example, measures for the operator might be the number of prints over some time interval, a certain grade on a test during his training and attendance recorded on attendance sheets to his Quality Circle.

   Identifying which measures to take is often the toughest part of the performance management process. You have to look at the appropriate level or domain in the organisation, its desired results, and consider what are the most valid, reliable and practical measurements to use. With complex and rapidly changing domains, it often helps to identify outcome and driver measures, and patterns of effects.

6. *Identify more specific measures for each first-level measure if necessary*: For example, regarding the

operator's measure for operating his machine, he may have to produce at least 500 high-quality prints an hour for eight hours, Monday through Friday during the fiscal year. High-quality means no smears or tears. The Director of the Catalogue Department evaluates whether the operator made this goal or not.

7. *Identify standards for evaluating how well the domain's desired results were achieved*: Standards specify how well a result should be achieved. For example, the operator "meets expectations" if the Director of the Catalogue Department agrees that the operator produced 500 high-quality prints an hour for eight hours, Monday through Friday during the fiscal year. If he produces 600, he "exceeds expectations", 700 is "superior performance", 400 is "does not meet expectation", etc.

8. *Document a performance plan - including desired results, measures and standards*: The performance plan describes the domain's preferred results, how results tie back to the organisation's results, weighting of results, how results will be measured and what standards are used to evaluate results. Developing the plan is often the responsibility of the head of the domain. However, the plan should be developed as much as possible with participants in the domain.

Development of the Performance Plan typically includes the first eight steps of the basic 14 steps in performance management. The Performance Appraisal picks up from step nine. Here also continue the example of the machine operator. At this point in this example, the Performance Plan has been developed. Information is here generic to performance management, that is, the information generally applies to any performance management effort, e.g., organisation, process, subsystem or employee.

9. *Conduct ongoing observations and measurements to track performance:* The operator's supervisor would observe the number of high-quality prints, including staying in contact with the Director of the Catalogue Department.

10. *Exchange ongoing feedback about performance:* Feedback is information relevant to how well results are being achieved. Useful feedback is timely, feasible and understood. Ideally, feedback address key activities to improve or reinforce performance. Usually, the larger the number of sources giving feedback, the more accurate is the depiction of events. In our example, the employee, supervisor and Director of the Catalogue Department should continue to share impressions of how well results are being achieved. Any ideas to improve or support performance should be implemented as appropriate. This ongoing feedback is often one of the most important aspects of performance management.

11. *Conduct a performance appraisal:* A performance appraisal includes documentation of expected results, standards of performance, progress toward achieving of results, how well they were achieved, examples indicating achievement, suggestions to improve performance and how those suggestions can be followed. In example, the appraisal should include input from the employee, supervisor and Director of the Catalogue Department. The performance appraisal should be carried out at regular intervals as performance tracking is underway.

12. *If performance meets desired performance standards, reward for performance*: In the example, the machine operator may be due some form of reward, that is, recognition or compensation, e.g., letter of recognition, promotion, letter of commendation, etc. This step in the performance management process is often overlooked when focusing on organisation-wide performance improvement, or on a major subsystem.

6.4. BENEFITS OF PERFORMANCE MANAGEMENT

PM focuses on results, rather than behaviours and activities: A common misconception among supervisors is that behaviours and activities are the same as results. Thus, an employee may appear extremely busy, but not be contributing at all toward the goals of the organisation. An example is the employee who manually reviews completion of every form and procedure, rather than supporting automation of the review. The supervisor may conclude the employee is very committed to the organisation and works very hard, thus, deserving a very high performance rating.

Aligns organisational activities and processes to the goals of the organisation: PM identifies organisational goals, results needed to achieve those goals, measures of effectiveness or efficiency (outcomes) toward the goals, and means (drivers) to achieve the goals. This chain of measurements is examined to ensure alignment with overall results of the organisation.

Produces meaningful measurements: These measurements have a wide variety of useful applications. They are useful in benchmarking, or setting standards for comparison with best practices in other organisations. They provide consistent basis for comparison during internal change efforts. They indicate results during improvement efforts, such as employee training, management development, quality programmes, etc. They help ensure equitable and fair treatment to employees based on performance.

Other benefits of Performance Management (PM):

— Helps you think about what results you really want. You're forced to be accountable, to "put a stake in the ground".

— Depersonalises issues. Supervisor's focus on behaviours and results, rather than personalities.

— Validates expectations. In today's age of high expectations when organisations are striving to transform themselves and society, having measurable results can verify whether grand visions are realistic or not.

— Helps ensure equitable treatment of employees because appraisals are based on results.

— Optimises operations in the organisation because goals and results are more closely aligned.

— Cultivates a change in perspective from activities to results.

— Performance reviews are focused on contributions to the organisational goals, e.g., forms include the question "What organisational goal were contributed to and how?"

— Supports ongoing communication, feedback and dialogue about organisational goals. Also supports communication between employee and supervisor.

— Performance is seen as an ongoing process, rather than a one-time, shapshot event.

— Provokes focus on the needs of customers, whether internal or external.

— Cultivates a systems perspective, that is, focus on the relationships and exchanges between subsystems, e.g., departments, processes, teams and employees. Accordingly, personnel focus on patterns and themes in the organisation, rather than specific events.

— Continuing focus and analysis on results helps to correct several myths, e.g., "learning means results", "job satisfaction produces productivity", etc.

— Produces specificity in commitments and resources.

— Provides specificity for comparisons, direction and planning.

Typical concerns expressed about performance management are that it seems extraordinarily difficult and often unreliable to measure phenomena as complex as performance. People point out that today's organisations are rapidly changing, thus results and measures quickly become obsolete. They add that translating human desires and interactions to measurements is impersonal and even heavy handed.

When performance management is carried out with an employee, filling out the performance form and having the performance discussion is not the highlight of the performance process — the highlight has been occurring during the year when the supervisor and employee exchanged ongoing feedback about performance. Filling out the form and having the discussion are really measurements, too. If the performance process is done well, the performance review discussion should include absolutely no surprises for the employee. All feedback to him or her already should have occurred.

7

HOW TO DESIGN MY ORGANISATION

Managing a successful business—or building up the health of an already established business — requires healthy, ongoing leadership and management, planning, product and service development, marketing and financial management. To carry out these practices in a healthy manner, it's important to first understand the basic "territory" in which these practices are carried out. These practices are all "systems" that occur within the larger system of the organisation. This is not academic talk — this is a highly practical point to understand.

To truly understand and be effective at these practices, it helps greatly if leaders, managers and employees have some basic understanding of the overall "system" of the business, its common traits, dimensions, "personalities" and life cycles. Too often, this basic nature is not understood. Instead, people tend to focus only on the day-to-day events and when problems occur, they don't see the "larger picture" in order to resolve these problems effectively.

Basically, an organisation is a group of people intentionally organised to accomplish an overall, common goal or set of goals. Business organisations can range in size from two people to tens of thousands. There are several important aspects to consider about the goal of the business organisation. These features are explicit (deliberate and recognised) or implicit (operating unrecognised, "behind the scenes"). Ideally, these features are carefully considered and established, usually during the strategic planning process.

— *Vision*: Members of the organisation often have some image in their minds about how the organisation should be working, how it should appear when things are going well.

— *Mission*: An organisation operates according o an overall purpose, or mission.

— *Values*: All organisations operate according to overall values, or priorities in the nature of how they carry out their activities. These values are the personality, or culture, of the organisation.

— *Strategic Goals*: Organisations members often work to achieve several overall accomplishments, or goals, as they work toward their mission.

— *Strategies*: Organisations usually follow several overall general approaches to reach their goals.

Organisations have major subsystems, such as departments, programs, divisions, teams, eta. Each of these subsystems has a way of doing things to, along with other subsystems, achieve the overall goals of the organisation. Often, these systems and processes are define by plans, policies and procedures. How you interpret each of the above major parts of an organisation depends very much on your values and your nature. People can view organisations as machines, organisms, families, groups, eta.

7.1. ORGANISATIONS AS SYSTEMS

A system is a collection of parts integrated to accomplish

an overall goal (a system of people is an organisation). Systems have input, processes, outputs and outcomes, with ongoing feedback among these various parts. If one part of the system is removed, the nature of the system is changed. Systems range from very simple to very complex. There are numerous types of systems. Complex systems, such as social systems, are comprised of numerous subsystems, as well. These subsystems are arranged in hierarchies, and integrated to accomplish the overall goal of the overall system.

Each subsystem has its own boundaries of sorts, and includes various inputs, processes, outputs and outcomes geared to accomplish an overall goal for the subsystem. A pile of sand is not a system. If one removes a sand particle, you've still got a pile of sand. However, a functioning car is a system. Remove the carburetor and you've no longer got a working car.

Recently, management studies has come to view organisations from a new perspective: a systems perspective. This systems perspective may seem quite basic. Yet, decades of management training and practices in the workplace have not followed from this perspective. Only recently, with tremendous changes facing organisations and how they operate, have educators and managers come to face this new way of looking at things. This interpretation has brought about a significant change (or paradigm shift) in the way management studies and approaches organisations.

The effect of this systems theory in management is that writers, educators, consultants, etc. are helping managers to look at organisations from a broader perspective. Systems theory has brought a new perspective for managers to interpret patterns and events in their organisations. In the past, managers typically took one part and focused on that. Then they moved all attention to another part. The problem was that an organisation could, e.g., have wonderful departments that operate well by themselves but don't integrate well together. Consequently, the organisation suffers as a whole. Now, more managers are recognising the various parts of the organisation, and, in particular, the interrelations of the parts, e.g., the coordination of central offices with other departments, engineering with manufacturing, supervisors with workers, etc.

Managers now focus more attention on matters of ongoing organisation and feedback. Managers now diagnose problems, not by examining what appear to be separate pieces of the organisation, but by recognising larger patterns of interactions. Managers maintain perspective by focusing on the outcomes they want from their organisations. Now managers focus on structures that provoke behaviours that determine events — rather than reacting to events as was always done in the past.

7.2. ORGANISATION DESIGN

Organisation design is a formal, guided process for integrating the people, information and technology of an organisation. It is used to match the form of the organisation as closely as possible to the purpose(s) the organisation seeks to achieve. Through the design process, organisations act to improve the probability that the collective efforts of members will be successful. Typically, design is approached as an internal change under the guidance of an external facilitator. Managers and members work together to define the needs of the organisation then create systems to meet those needs most effectively. The facilitator assures that a systematic process is followed and encourages creative thinking.

7.2.1. Hierarchical Systems

Most organisations today are designed as a bureaucracy

in which authority and responsibility are arranged in a hierarchy. Within the hierarchy rules, policies, and procedures are uniformly and impersonally applied to exert control over member behaviours. Activity is organised within sub-units in which people perform specialised functions such as manufacturing, sales, or accounting. People who perform similar tasks are clustered together. The same basic organisational form is *assumed* to be appropriate for any organisation, be it a government, school, business, church, or fraternity. It is familiar, predictable, and rational.

As familiar and rational as the functional hierarchy may be, there are distinct disadvantages to blindly applying the same form of organisation to all purposeful groups. To understand the problem, begin by observing that different groups wish to achieve different outcomes. Second, observe that different groups have different members, and that each group possesses a different culture. These differences in desired outcomes, and in people, should alert us to the danger of assuming there is any single best way of organising. To be complete, however, also observe that different groups will likely choose different methods through which they will achieve their purpose. Service groups will choose different methods than manufacturing groups, and both will choose different methods than groups whose purpose is primarily social. One structure cannot possibly fit all.

7.2.2. Design Process

Organisation design begins with the creation of a strategy — a set of decision guidelines by which members will choose appropriate actions. The strategy is derived from clear, concise statements of purpose, and vision, and from the organisation's basic philosophy. Strategy unifies the intent of the organisation and focuses members toward actions designed to accomplish desired outcomes. The strategy encourages actions that support the purpose and discourages those that do not. Creating a strategy is planning, not organising. To organise we must connect people with each other in meaningful and purposeful ways.

Further, we must connect people with the information and technology necessary for them to be successful. Organisation structure defines the formal relationships among people and specifies both their roles and their responsibilities. Administrative systems govern the organisation through guidelines, procedures and policies. Information and technology define the process(es) through which members achieve outcomes. Each element must support each of the others and together they must support the organisation's purpose.

Organisations are an invention of man. They are contrived social systems through which groups seek to exert influence or achieve a stated purpose. People choose to organise when they recognise that by acting alone they are limited in their ability to achieve. When we organise we seek to direct, or pattern, the activities of a group of people toward a common outcome. How this pattern is designed and implemented greatly influences effectiveness. Patterns of activity that are complementary and interdependent are more likely to result in the achievement of intended outcomes. In contrast, activity patterns that are unrelated and independent are more likely to produce unpredictable, and often unintended results.

The process of organisation design matches people, information, and technology to the purpose, vision, and strategy of the organisation. Structure is designed to enhance communication and information flow among people. Systems are designed to encourage individual responsibility and decision making. Technology is used to enhance human capabilities to accomplish meaningful work. The end product is an integrated system of people and resources, tailored to the specific direction of the organisation.

7.3. NEW ORGANISATIONAL STRUCTURES

Network Structure: This modern structure includes the linking of numerous, separate organisations to optimise their interaction in order to accomplish a common, overall goal. An example is a joint venture to build a complex, technical systems such as the space shuttle. Another example is a network of construction companies to build a large structure.

Virtual Organisation: This emerging form is based on organisation members interacting with each other completely, or almost completely, via telecommunications. Members may never actually meet each other.

Self-Managed Teams: These teams usually include from 5-15 people and are geared to produce a product or service. Members provide a range of the skills needed to produce the product. The team is granted sufficient authority and access to resources to produce their product in a timely fashion. The hallmark of a self-managed team is that members indeed manage their own group, i.e., they manage access to resources, scheduling, supervision, etc. Team members develop their own process for identifying and rotating members in managerial roles. Often, authority at any given time rests with whomever has the most expertise about the current activity or task in the overall project. Often members are trained in various problem-solving techniques and team-building techniques.

These teams work best in environments where the technologies to deliver the product or service are highly complex and the marketplace and organisation environments are continually changing. Self-managed teams pose a unique challenge for the traditional manager. It can be extremely difficult for him or her to support empowerment of the self-managed team, taking the risk of letting go of his or her own control.

Learning Organisations: In an environment where environments are continually changing, it's critical that organisations detect and quickly correct its own errors. This requires continuous feedback to, and within, the organisation. Continual feedback allows the organisation to 'unlearn' old beliefs and remain open to new feedback, uncoloured by long-held beliefs. In a learning organisation, managers don't direct as much as they facilitate the workers' applying new information and learning from that experience. Managers ensure time to exchange feedback, to inquire and reflect about the feedback, and then to gain consensus on direction.

Self-Organising Systems: Self-organising systems have the ability to continually change their structure and internal processes to conform to feedback with the environment. A self-organising system requires a strong current goal or purpose. It requires continual feedback with its surrounding environment.

It requires continual reference to a common set of values and dialoguing around these values. It requires continued and shared reflection around the system's current processes. The manager of this type of organisation requires high value on communication and a great deal of patience — and the ability to focus on outcomes rather than outputs. Focus is more on learning than on method.

7.3.1. New Nature of Organisations

New forms of organisations are geared to make organisations more receptive, adaptive and generative — always focused on meeting the needs of stakeholders. New forms of organisations often exhibit the following characteristics:

— *Strong employee involvement*: input to the system starts from those closest to the outcome preferred by the system, from those most in-the-know about whether the organisation is achieving its preferred outcomes with its stakeholders or not. This way, the organisation stays highly attuned and adaptive to the needs of stakeholders.

— *Organic in nature*: less rules and regulations, sometimes no clear boundaries and always-changing forms

— *Authority based on capability*: ensures the organisation remains a means to an end and not an end in itself

— *Alliances*: takes advantage of economies of scale, e.g., collaborations, networks, strategic alliances/ mergers, etc.

— *Teams*: shares activities to take advantage of economies of scale at the lowest levels of activities and ensures full involvement of employees at the lowest levels

— *Flatter, decentralised organisations*: less middle management, resulting in top management exchanging more feedback with those providing products and services; also results in less overhead costs

— *Mindfulness of environments, changes, patterns and themes*: priority on reflection and inquiry to learn from experience; develop "learning organisations"

7.4. ORGANISATIONAL CULTURE

Basically, organisational culture is the personality of the organisation. Culture is comprised of the assumptions, values, norms and tangible signs (artifacts) of organisation members and their behaviours. Members of an organisation soon come to sense the particular culture of an organisation. Culture is one of those terms that's difficult to express distinctly, but everyone knows it when they sense it. Corporate culture can be looked at as a system. Inputs include feedback from, e.g., society, professions, laws, stories, heroes, values on competition or service, etc. The process is based on our assumptions, values and norms, e.g., our values on money, time, facilities, space and people. Outputs or effects of our culture are, e.g., organisational behaviours, technologies, strategies, image, products, services, appearance, etc.

The concept of culture is particularly important when attempting to manage organisation-wide change. Practitioners are coming to realise that, despite the best-laid plans, organisational change must include not only changing structures and processes, but also changing the corporate culture as well. There's been a great deal of literature generated over the past decade about the concept of organisational culture — particularly in regard to learning how to change organisational culture.

Organisational change efforts are rumoured to fail the vast majority of the time. Usually, this failure is credited to lack of understanding about the strong role of culture and the role it plays in organisations. That's one of the reasons that many strategic planners now place as much emphasis on identifying strategic values as they do mission and vision.

Academy Culture: Employees are highly skilled and tend to stay in the organisation, while working their way up the ranks. The organisation provides a stable environment in which employees can development and exercise their skills. Examples are universities, hospitals, large corporations, etc.

Baseball Team Culture: Employees are "free agents" who have highly prized skills. They are in high demand and can rather easily get jobs elsewhere. This type of culture exists in fast-paced, high-risk organisations, such as investment banking, advertising, etc.

Club Culture: The most important requirement for employees in this culture is to fit into the group. Usually employees start at the bottom and stay with the organisation. The organisation promotes from within and highly values seniority. Examples are the military, some law firms, etc.

7.5. ORGANISATIONAL CHANGE

Typically, the concept of organisational change is in regard to organisation-wide change, as opposed to smaller changes such as adding a new person, modifying a program, etc. Examples of organisation-wide change might include a change in mission, restructuring operations (e.g., restructuring to self-managed teams, layoffs, etc.), new technologies, mergers, major collaborations, "rightsising", new programs such as Total Quality Management, re-engineering, etc. Typically there are strong resistances to change.

People are afraid of the unknown. Many people think things are already just fine and don't understand the need for change. Many are inherently cynical about change, particularly from reading about the notion of "change" as if it's a mantra. Many doubt there are effective means to accomplish major organisational change. Often there are conflicting goals in the organisation, e.g., to increase resources to accomplish the change yet concurrently cut costs to remain viable.

Organisation-wide change often goes against the very values held dear by members in the organisation, that is, the change may go against how members believe things should be done. That's why much of organisational-change literature discusses needed changes in the culture of the organisation, including changes in members' values and beliefs and in the way they enact these values and beliefs.

Successful change must involve top management, including the board and chief executive. Usually there's a champion who initially instigates the change by being visionary, persuasive and consistent. A change agent role is usually responsible to translate the vision to a realistic plan and carry out the plan. Change is usually best carried out as a team-wide effort. Communications about the change should be frequent and with all organisation members. To sustain change, the structures of the organisation itself should be modified, including strategic plans, policies and procedures.

This change in the structures of the organisation typically involves an unfreezing, change and re-freezing process. The best approaches to address resistances is through increased and sustained communications and education.

8

HOW TO BECOME
AN EFFECTIVE LEADER

The basis of good leadership is honourable character and selfless service to your organisation. In your employees' eyes, your leadership is everything you do that effects the organisation's objectives and their well being. Respected leaders concentrate on what they are, what they know and what they do. People want to be guided by those they respect and who have a clear sense of direction. To gain respect, they must be ethical. A sense of direction is achieved by conveying a strong vision of the future.

The two most important keys to effective leadership are:

1. Trust and confidence in top leadership was the single most reliable predictor of employee satisfaction in an organisation.

2. Effective communication by leadership in three critical areas was the key to winning organisational trust and confidence:

   a. Helping employees understand the company's overall business strategy.

   b. Helping employees understand how they contribute to achieving key business objectives.

    c. Sharing information with employees on both how the company is doing and how an employee's own division is doing - relative to strategic business objectives.

8.1. LEADERSHIP PRINCIPLES

1. *Be technically proficient*: As a leader, you must know your job and have a solid familiarity with your employees' tasks.

2. *Seek responsibility and take responsibility for your actions* - Search for ways to guide your organisation to new heights. And when things go wrong, they always do sooner or later — do not blame others. Analyse the situation, take corrective action, and move on to the next challenge.

3. *Make sound and timely decisions* - Use good problem solving, decision making, and planning tools.

4. *Set the example*: Be a good role model for your employees. They must not only hear what they are expected to do, but also see. We must become the change we want to see - Mahatma Gandhi

5. *Know your people and look out for their well-being*: Know human nature and the importance of sincerely caring for your workers.

6. *Keep your workers informed*: Know how to communicate with not only them, but also seniors and other key people.

7. *Develop a sense of responsibility in your workers*: Help to develop good character traits that will help them carry out their professional responsibilities.

8. *Ensure that tasks are understood, supervised, and accomplished:* Communication is the key to this responsibility.

9. *Train as a team:* **Although** many so called leaders call their organisation, department, section, etc. a team; they are not really teams...they are just a group of people doing their jobs.

10. *Use the full capabilities of your organisation* - By developing a team spirit, you will be able to employ your organisation, department, section, etc. to its fullest capabilities.

8.2. LEADERSHIP FACTORS

There are four major factors in leadership:

8.2.1. Follower

Different people require different styles of leadership. For example, a new hire requires more supervision than an experienced employee. A person who lacks motivation requires a different approach than one with a high degree of motivation. You must know your people! The fundamental starting point is having a good understanding of human nature, such as needs, emotions, and motivation. You must become to know your employees' be, know, and do attributes.

8.2.2. Leader

You must have a honest understanding of who you are, what you know, and what you can do. Also, note that it is the followers, not the leader who determines if a leader is successful. If they do not trust or lack confidence in their leader, then they will be uninspired. To be successful you have to convince your followers, not yourself or your superiors, that you are worthy of being followed.

8.2.3. Communication

You lead through two-way communication. Much of it is nonverbal. For instance, when you "set the example," that communicates to your people that you would not ask them to perform anything that you would not be willing to do. What and how you communicate either builds or harms the relationship between you and your employees.

8.2.4. Situation

All are different. What you do in one situation will not always work in another. You must use your judgment to decide the best course of action and the leadership style needed for each situation. For example, you may need to confront an employee for inappropriate behavior, but if the confrontation is too late or too early, too harsh or too weak, then the results may prove ineffective. Various forces will affect these factors. Examples of forces are your relationship with your seniors, the skill of your people, the informal leaders within your organisation, and how your company is organised.

8.3. HOW TO LEAD EFFECTIVELY

Your thinking skills can be considered directional skills because they set the direction for your organisation. They provide vision, purpose, and goal definition. These are your eyes and ears to the future, allowing you to recognise the need for change, when to make it, how to implement it, and how to manage it. You find vision by reaching for any available reason to change, grow, and improve. Just as you perform preventive maintenance on your car, you must perform preventive maintenance on your organisation. Treat every project as a change effort. Treat every job as a new learning experience. Good organisations convey a strong vision of where they will be in the future. As a leader, you have to get your people to trust you and be sold on your vision.

When setting goals, keep these points in mind:

1. They should be realistic and attainable.

2. They should improve the organisation (moral, monetary, etc.).

3. All the people should be involved in the goal-setting process.

4. A programme should be developed to achieve each goal.

There are four characteristics of goal setting:

1. *Goal Difficulty*: Increasing your employees' goal difficulty increases their challenges and enhances the amount of effort expended to achieve them. The more difficult goals lead to increased performance if they seem feasible. If they seem too high, employees will give up when they fail to achieve them.

2. *Goal Specificity*: When given specific goals, employees tend to perform higher. Telling them to do their best or giving no guidance increases ambiguity about what is expected. Employees need a set goal or model in order to display the correct behavior.

3. *Feedback*: Providing feedback enhances the effects of goal setting. Performance feedback keeps their behavior directed on the right target and encourages them to work harder to achieve the goal.

4. *Participation in Goal Setting*: Employees who participate in the process, generally set higher goals than if the goals were set for them. It also affects their belief that the goals are obtainable and increases their motivation to achieve them.

8.4. SUPERVISING

Supervision is keeping a grasp on the situation and ensuring that plans and policies are implemented properly. It includes giving instructions and inspecting the accomplishment of a task. There is a narrow band of adequate supervision. On one side of the band is over-supervision; and on the other side is under-supervision. Over-supervision stifles initiative, breeds resentment, and lowers morale and motivation. Under-supervision leads to miscommunication, lack of coordination, and the perception by subordinates that the leader does not care. All employees benefit from appropriate supervision by seniors with more knowledge and experience who tend to see the situation more objectively.

Evaluating is part of supervising is defined as judging the worth, quality, or significance of people, ideas, or things. It includes looking at the ways people are accomplishing a task. It means getting feedback on how well something is being done and interpreting that feedback. People need feedback so that they judge their performance. Without it, they will keep performing tasks wrong, or stop performing the steps that makes their work great.

Use checklists to list tasks that need to be accomplished. Almost all of us have poor memories when it comes to remembering a list of details. List tasks by priorities. Double check on important things by following through. Strange things can happen if you are not aware of them. Paperwork gets lost, plans get changed, and people forget. If you have a system of checks and double checks, you will discover mistakes, have time to correct them, and minimise any disruptions. Following through may seem to be a waste of your time and energy, but in the long run, it pays off. You will spend less time and energy correcting mistakes and omissions made long ago.

8.4.1. Inspiring Your Employees

Getting people to accomplish something is much easier if they have the inspiration to do so. Inspire means "to breathe life into." And in order to perform that, we have to have some life ourselves. Three main actions will aid you in accomplishing this:

1. *Be passionate*: In organisations where the is a leader with great enthusiasm about a project, a trickle-down effect will occur. You must be committed to the work you are doing. If you do not communicate excitement, how can you expect your people to get worked up about it?

2. *Get your employees involved in the decision making process*: People who are involved in the decision making process participate much more enthusiastically than those who just carry out their boss's order. Help them contribute and tell them you value their opinions. Listen to them and incorporate their ideas when it makes sense to so.

3. Know what your organisation is about!: A leader's primary responsibility is to develop people and enable them to reach their full potential. Your people may come from diverse backgrounds, but they all have goals they want to accomplish. Create a "people environment" where they truly can be all they can be.

8.4.2. Training and Coaching

As a leader you must view coaching from two different viewpoints: 1) Coaching to lead others. 2) Being coached to achieve self-improvement. Training and coaching are two different things, although some people use them interchangeably. Training is a structured lesson designed to provide the employee with the knowledge and skills to perform a task. Coaching, on the other hand, is a process designed to help the employee gain greater competence and to overcome barriers so as to improve job performance.

Training and coaching go hand-in-hand. First you train them with lots of technical support, and then you coach them with motivational pointers. Both training and coaching help to create the conditions that cause someone to learn and develop. People learn by the examples of others, by forming a picture in their minds of what they are trying to learn, by gaining and understanding necessary information, by applying it to their job, or practice.

8.5. POWER OF LEADERSHIP

Leadership power is much more than the use of force...it is influencing others to truly WANT to achieve a goal. Plain power forces others to achieve a goal. Power refers to a capacity or potential as it implies a potential that need not be actualised to be effective. That is, a power may exist, but does not have to be used to be effective. For example, an officer in the Army has certain powers over enlisted personal, but that power does not have to used to be effective. The mere knowledge of an officer's power by an enlisted person has some influence over him or her.

A person has the potential for influencing five points of power over another:

1. *Coercive Power*: Power that is based on fear. A person with coercive power can make things difficult for people. These are the persons that you want to avoid getting angry. Employees working under coercive managers are unlikely to be committed, and more likely to resist the manager.

2. *Reward Power*: Compliance achieved based on the ability to distribute rewards that others view as valuable. Able to give special benefits or rewards to people. You might find it advantageous to trade favours with him or her.

3. *Legitimate Power*: The power a person receives as a result of his or her position in the formal hierarchy of an organisation. The person has the right, considering his or her position and your job responsibilities, to expect you to comply with legitimate requests.

4. *Expert Power*: Influence based on special skills or knowledge. This person earns respect by experience and knowledge. Expert power is the most strongly and consistently related to effective employee performance.

5. *Referent Power*: Influence based on possession by an individual or desirable resources or personal traits. You like the person and enjoy doing things for him or her.

8.6. MODELS OF LEADERSHIP

Leadership models help to understand what makes leaders act the way they do. The ideal is not to lock yourself in to a type of behavior discussed in the model, but to realise that every situation calls for a different approach or behavior to be taken. Two models are the Four Framework Approach and the Managerial Grid.

8.5.1. Four Framework Approach

Leaders display leadership behaviours in one of four types of frameworks:

Structural Framework: In an effective leadership situation, the leader is a social architect whose leadership style is analysis and design. While in an ineffective leadership situation, the leader is a petty tyrant whose leadership style is details. Structural Leaders focus on structure, strategy, environment, implementation, experimentation, and adaptation.

Human Resource Framework: In an effective leadership situation, the leader is a catalyst and servant whose leadership style is support, advocate, and empowerment. While in an ineffective leadership situation, the leader is a pushover, whose leadership style is abdication and fraud. Human Resource Leaders believe in people and communicate that belief; they are visible and accessible; they empower, increase participation, support, share information, and move decision making down into the organisation.

Political Framework: In an effective leadership situation, the leader is an advocate, whose leadership style is coalition and building. While in an ineffective leadership situation, the leader is a hustler, whose leadership style is manipulation. Political leaders clarify what they want and what they can get; they assess the distribution of power and interests; they build linkages to other stakeholders, use persuasion first, then use negotiation and coercion only if necessary.

Symbolic Framework: In an effective leadership situation, the leader is a prophet, whose leadership style is inspiration. While in an ineffective leadership situation, the leader is a fanatic or fool, whose leadership style is smoke and mirrors. Symbolic leaders view organisations as a stage or theatre to play certain roles and give impressions; these leaders use symbols to capture attention; they try to frame experience by providing plausible interpretations of experiences; they discover and communicate a vision. This model suggests that leaders can be put into one of these four categories and there are times when one approach is appropriate and times when it would not be. Any one of these approaches alone would be inadequate, thus we should strive to be conscious of all four approaches, and not just rely on one or two.

8.5.2. Managerial Grid

Managerial Grid uses two axis:

1. Concern for people" is plotted using the vertical axis

2. Concern for task" is along the horizontal axis.

8.5.2.1 Types of Leaders

1. *Authoritarian Leader (high task, low relationship)*: People who get this rating are very much task oriented and are hard on their workers (autocratic). There is little or no allowance for cooperation or collaboration. Heavily task oriented people display these characteristics: they are very strong on schedules; they expect people to do what they are told without question or debate; when something goes wrong they tend to focus on who is to blame rather than concentrate on exactly what is wrong and how to prevent it; they are intolerant of what they see as dissent, so it is difficult for their subordinates to contribute or develop.

2. *Team Leader (high task, high relationship)*: This type of person leads by positive example and endeavours to foster a team environment in which all team members can reach their highest potential, both as team members and as people. They encourage the team to reach team goals as effectively as possible, while also working tirelessly to strengthen the bonds among the various members. They normally form and lead some of the most productive teams.

3. *Country Club Leader (low task, high relationship)*: This person uses predominantly reward power to maintain discipline and to encourage the team to accomplish its goals. Conversely, they are almost incapable of employing the more punitive coercive and legitimate powers. This inability results from fear that using such powers could jeopardise relationships with the other team members.

4. *Impoverished Leader (low task, low relationship)*: A leader who uses a "delegate and disappear" management style. Since they are not committed to either task accomplishment or maintenance; they essentially allow their team to do whatever it wishes and prefer to detach themselves from the team process by allowing the team to suffer from a series of power struggles.

9

CONTROLLING AND COORDINATING

Organisational coordination and control is taking a systematic approach to figuring out if you're doing what you wanted to be doing or not. It's the part of planning after you've decided what you wanted to be doing.

9.1. MANAGEMENT CONTROL

Many people assert that as the nature of organisations has changed, so must the nature of management control. Some people go so far as to claim that management shouldn't exercise any form of control whatsoever. They claim that management should exist to support employee's efforts to be fully productive members of organisations and communities — therefore, any form of control is completely counterproductive to management and employees.

Some people even react strongly against the phrase "management control". The word itself can have a negative connotation, e.g., it can sound dominating, coercive and heavy-handed. It seems that writers of management literature now prefer use of the term "coordinating" rather than "controlling".

9.2. ORGANISATIONAL COORDINATION

Regardless of the negative connotation of the word "control", it must exist or there is no organisation at all. In its most basic form, an organisation is two or more people working together to reach a goal. Whether an organisation is highly bureaucratic or changing and self-organising, the organisation must exist for some reason, some purpose, some mission (implicit or explicit)—or it isn't an organisation at all.

The organisation must have some goal. Identifying this goal requires some form of planning, informal or formal. Reaching the goal means identifying some strategies, formal or informal. These strategies are agreed upon by members of the organisation through some form of communication, formal or informal. Then members set about to act in accordance with what they agreed to do. They may change their minds, fine. But they need to recognise and acknowledge that they're changing their minds. This form of ongoing communication to reach a goal, tracking activities toward the goal and then subsequent decisions about what to do is the essence of management coordination. It needs to exist in some manner — formal or informal.

Typical methods of coordination in organisations are used as means to communicate direction and guide behaviours in that direction. The function of these methods is not to "control", but rather to guide. If, from ongoing communications among management and employees, the direction changes, then fine.

Organisations often use standardised documents to ensure complete and consistent information is gathered. Documents include titles and dates to detect different versions of the document. Computers have revolutionised administrative controls through use of integrated management information systems, project management software, human resource information systems, office automation software, etc. Organisations typically require a wide range of reports, e.g., financial reports, status reports, project reports, etc. to monitor what's being done, by when and how.

9.3. DELEGATION

Delegation is an approach to get things done, in conjunction with other employees. Delegation is often viewed as a major means of influence and therefore is categorised as an activity in leading. Delegation generally includes assigning responsibility to an employee to complete a task, granting the employee sufficient authority to gain the resources to do the task and letting the employee decide how that task will be carried out. Typically, the person assigning the task shares accountability with the employee for ensuring the task is completed.

Delegating involves working with an employee to establish goals, granting them sufficient authority and responsibility to achieve the goals, often giving them substantial freedom in deciding how the goals will be achieved, remaining available as a resource to help them achieve the goals, assessing their performance addressing performance issues and/or rewarding their performance. Ultimately, the supervisor retains responsibility for the attainment of the goals, but chooses to achieve the goals by delegating to someone else.

Delegation can sometimes be a major challenge for new supervisors to learn because they are concerned about giving up control or struggle to have confidence in the abilities of others. Supervisors that can effectively delegate can free up a great deal of their own time, help their direct reports to cultivate expertise in learning, and can develop their own leadership skills — skills that are critical for problem solving, goal attainment and learning. The hallmark of good supervision is effective delegation.

Delegation is when supervisors give responsibility and authority to subordinates to complete a task. Effective delegation develops people who are ultimately more fulfilled and productive. Managers become more fulfilled and productive themselves as they learn to count on their staffs and are freed up to attend to more strategic issues. Delegation is often very difficult for new supervisors, particularly if they have had to scramble to start the nonprofit or start a major new service themselves.

Many managers want to remain comfortable, making the same decisions they have always made. They believe they can do a better job themselves. They don't want to risk losing any of their power and stature. Often, they don't want to risk giving authority to subordinates in case they fail and impair the organisation. However, there are basic approaches to delegation that, with practice, become the backbone of effective supervision and development.

9.3.1. General Steps to Accomplish Delegation

1. *Delegate the whole task to one person.* This gives the person the responsibility and increases their motivation.

2. *Select the right person.* Assess the skills and capabilities of subordinates and assign the task to the most appropriate one.

3. *Clearly specify your preferred results.* Give information on what, why, when, who, where and how. Write this information down.

4. *Delegate responsibility and authority — assign the task, not the method to accomplish it.* Let the subordinate

complete the task in the manner they choose, as long as the results are what the supervisor specifies. Let the employee have strong input as to the completion date of the project. Note that you may not even know how to complete the task yourself — this is often the case with higher levels of management.

5. Ask the employee to summarise back to you, their impressions of the project and the results you prefer.

6. *Get ongoing non-intrusive feedback about progress on the project.* This is a good reason to continue to get weekly, written status reports from all direct reports. Reports should cover what they did last week, plan to do next week and any potential issues. Regular staff meetings provide this ongoing feedback, as well.

7. *Maintain open lines of communication.* Don't hover over the subordinate, but sense what they're doing and support their checking in with you along the way.

8. *If you're not satisfied with the progress, don't immediately take the project back.* Continue to work with the employee and ensure they perceive the project as their responsibility.

9. *Evaluate and reward performance.* Evaluate results, not methods. Address insufficient performance and reward successes.

9.4. EVALUATIONS

Evaluation is carefully collecting and analysing information in order to make decisions. There are many types of evaluations in organisations, for example, evaluation of marketing efforts, evaluation of employee performance, programme evaluations, etc. Evaluations can focus on many aspects of an organisation and its processes, for example, its goals, processes, outcomes, etc.

In the context of management activities evaluation is carefully collecting information about something in order to make necessary decisions about it. There are a large number and wide variety of evaluations that can occur in businesses, whether for-profit or nonprofit. Evaluation is closely related to performance management which includes identifying measures to indicate results. Evaluation often includes collecting information around these measures to conclude the extent of performance.

9.4.1. Evaluating Business Ideas and Products

Starting a business is easy: Deciding on what business to engage in is the difficult part. There are literally hundreds of ideas you might think of that could bring in extra income. Most home business entrepreneurs start-up with very little money and a strong belief that success will come to them if they work hard enough and offer a quality product or service. While this positive attitude is essential, it is not enough to guarantee financial success. A lot hinges on your management and marketing skills - and your product or service.

You can either choose a product-oriented or a service-oriented home business. A product-oriented business allows you to either create or manufacture the product yourself, or resell products that are made by others on a direct sales or drop-ship basis. On the other hand, you can opt to engage in a service-oriented business where you perform services at your home or perform services from home. Before you begin to develop your business idea, you need to determine its strength and viability. Ask yourself the following questions when evaluating an idea for a business or product:

1. *Does it satisfy or create a market need?* Introducing a new product without first testing the market is like jumping off a cliff blindfolded. In fact, many businesses fail because there is no adequate market for their products or services. Before you risk your resources on a new venture, it is necessary to get an objective picture of your prospective market. Although accurately determining the customer reaction to a new product is difficult, a new business owner must try to get hold of as much information on the market as he or she can either through a formal market research or through secondary research.

   The rule is find a need and fill it. To the extent possible, do not offer a product or service so new or unusual that people cannot understand why they should buy it - unless you want to spend most of your time and resources educating the public. Big companies, with their deep pockets, can afford to launch a massive educational campaign for breakthrough products. Home businesses, given their size and nature, often do not have the resources to mobilise such campaigns. Also, do not offer a product you love to make but whose market potential is weak at best.

2. *Will the product maintain market appeal?* Beware of fads and fleeting trends as these markets change quickly that your business cannot achieve a sufficient volume or a sufficient share of the market. If your product, however, is a fad, make sure that you can move fast enough to capitalise on it before it dies. Also determine if your product or service can be used nationally, or is it simply limited to your geographical area. With the increasing globalisation of business, you may need

to look at the international market and see if there is significant foreign competition.

3. *How unique is your product?* The goal is to be able to differentiate your product from your competitor. You need to show why your products and services are unique, distinct, or of considerably superior than your competitors. Every product in the world can be sold or presented in a new way. If you seriously intend to capture a significant market share, your potential customers must find more value from your product.

4. *How useful is your product?* Many new ideas and products are successful because their creators identified an unmet need in the market. Identify at the onset how your product or service will be used, and determine the frequency of product use. Some business ideas fill a real need, but in some cases the need have to be created through promotional advertising and promotions. This information can help build your marketing strategy.

5. *How much competition exists?* Remember, there is never a "no competition" situation. You product will always have its competition. Determine the kind of competition you will have — locally, regionally, and nationally. Look for heavy or moderate competition - the fact that competition exists in that market proves a demand, or at least a need for what you offer. However, test for market saturation. Unless you are offering a ground-breaking product, stay away from market with extremely few competitors.

Lack of competition could mean that your business idea is not profitable to begin with, or that your idea is so new and unique that no one has thought of it yet. Few players in the market could also imply that the market may be controlled by a monopoly or a cartel, the barriers to entry are too high for a small firm, or that the demand is too limited to sustain another entrant in the market

6. *Have you priced your product competitively?* The right price for a product or service is one of the essential elements in a solid business model. Don't do yourself injustice; the wrong price tag is like a ticket to disaster. Economic survival is the primary consideration underlying all pricing decisions. Ideally, a price should meet three requirements: it should match the competition; it should be attractive to your potential customers; and it should earn a profit for you. Set your prices, not by competition, but based on the needs of your business. Depending on your products, consider pricing yourself on the higher side: the higher you price yourself, the higher you position yourself.

7. *What is the level of difficulty in the creation or implementation of the product?* You need to consider the economic factors in the execution of the product, such as time, capital investment required, and marketing costs, personnel needed, among others. Also determine if you have the engineering, production, sales, and distribution facilities adequate for the product's impleme-ntation. You may have an excellent business idea, but if you do not have the economies of scale to produce it, then you might be better off to consider other products.

8. *What are the growth possibilities?* Your business model stands to succeed if the demand for your products or services can be expected to grow with a change in the economy. Check if your product can survive a major technological surge or obsolescence.

9. *Can I get backend sales?* Back-end sales are all the products or services you sell and resell to customers or clients after they have made their initial purchasing transaction with you. Determine if your product or service will warrant repeat sales. There is real business value in building a pool of repeat customers. The bulk of the sales, cash flow and current profit comes from utilising and then better utilising a back end.

10. *Is the product safe?* The safety of a product use is an important consideration for many consumers, particularly for manufactured products. If you are in the service business, you need to make sure that your personnel are properly trained with the goal of satisfying your customers foremost in their minds. Educate your consumers on how best to use the product and include clear instructions to avoid costly legal entanglements. Make sure that your business is insured against various forms of liabilities that may arise.

11. *Can my product be promoted with strong advertising copy?* Emotion sells. People are often motivated to buy a product or service because of some emotion, whether it is greed, fear or want. Response to advertisements often increases whenever you inject these elements into your ad. Sit down before you write the ad and ask yourself what you want to feel. Then translate these feelings to written words for your advertising copy. Stress what people can gain from ordering your product or service or tell them what they lose if they do not order.

12. *Will you be left with an inventory?* Avoid inventory risk; make sure that even you will buy the product. If you have inventory, consider getting homeowner's or renter's insurance policy to protect

your business against all possible disasters, be it fire, tornado, hurricane or earthquake

9.4.2. Financial Statements

As the money is spent, statements are changed to reflect what was spent, how it was spent and what it obtained. Review of financial statements is one of the more common methods to monitor the progress of programmes and plans. The most common financial statements include the balance sheet, income statement and cash flow statement. Financial audits are regularly conducted to ensure that financial management practices follow generally accepted standards, as well.

9.4.3. Performance Management

Performance management focuses on the performance of the total organisation, including its processes, critical subsystems and employees. Most of us have some basic impression of employee performance management, including the role of performance reviews. Performance reviews provide an opportunity for supervisors and their employees to regularly communicate about goals, how well those goals should be met, how well the goals are being met and what must be done to continue to meet (or change) those goals. The employee is rewarded in some form for meeting performance standards, or embarks on a development plan with the supervisor in order to improve performance.

9.4.4. Policies and Procedures

Policies help ensure that behaviours in the workplace conform to federal and state laws, and also to expectations of the organisation. Often, policies are applied to specified situations in the form of procedures.

Personnel policies and procedures help ensure that employee laws are followed and minimise the likelihood of costly litigation. A procedure is a step-by-step list of activities required to conduct a certain task. Procedures ensure that routine tasks are carried out in an effective and efficient fashion.

9.4.5. Quality Control and Operations Management

The concept of quality control has received a great deal of attention over the past twenty years. Many people recognise phrases such as "do it right the first time, "zero defects", "Total Quality Management", etc. Very broadly, quality includes specifying a performance standard monitoring and measuring results, comparing the results to the standard and then making adjusts as necessary. Recently, the concept of quality management has expanded to include organisation-wide programmes, such as Total Quality Management, ISO9000, Balanced Scorecard, etc. Operations management includes the overall activities involved in developing, producing and distributing products and services.

10

QUALITY CUSTOMER CONTACT

Today personal contact is lost in the shuffle. Warehouse stores sell their goods with almost no customer contact — maybe a 'thank you' at the checkout counter. Banks are finding certain customers want the contact with tellers even though it may be less efficient than an ATM machine. Handwritten letters carry a bigger impact than printed ones.

Many businesses have found that just technical skills are not enough. Businesses that compete directly against the mega-stores are finding that one competitive edge they have is in the personal contact area. Some companies have set up 'greeters' and 'service consultants' to try to keep the personal contact advantage. But a 'How are we doing today?' is not enough. When looking at quality personal contact be sure to look at these key areas:

1. *After the sale don't just say thanks and move along to something else.* Customers like to feel they are more than just a credit card or check. Take time to compliment their judgment and strike up a conversation showing interest in them personally. This is a very critical moment when a long term relationship can be established and reinforced.

2. *Correct mistakes in a timely manner even before the customer knows the mistake exists.* A proactive

approach shows the customer your real concern. Customers don't always expect perfection but they do expect you to "make it right".

3. *Use the customer's name if possible.* The greeter at WalMart can't do that. The Safeway clerk using your name after a credit card transaction is not the same either. To most people their name is one of the sweetest things they can hear. Use it!

4. *Measure customer satisfaction by surveys or direct conversation.* Those businesses that express interest in what their customers want demonstrate a caring attitude.

5. *Customer crises or emergencies provide an opportunity to establish a more permanent relationship.* Crises and emergencies make customers feel more vulnerable and this is an uncomfortable feeling. When a customer feels you went out of your way to help them when they needed it most they will not 'jump ship' if a competitor tries to steal them away.

6. *Add value to your product or service by doing something special even if it is a small thing.* Many of my clients in the auto repair industry do small things for their customers to keep them loyal. A two minute demonstration on how to change a fuse usually brings a 'thank you so very much for your concern' response. The customer may forget what they had fixed on their car that day but they will not forget how to change a fuse and who taught them.

7. *Stay relaxed and focus on the personal contact.* A business that presents a harried and anxious image implies that the business has internal problems. This does not create confidence and gives an otherwise good business a poor service image.

When used correctly quality customer contacts can create a true competitive advantage. With so many products and services becoming 'commoditised' the astute business owner and employee is always looking for ways to gain even a slight competitive advantage. Quality customer contacts enhance all the good value you give your customer.

There's a lot more to customer service than simply having a sign on your wall that says: "The customer is always right". For any business to be truly customer-focused, everyone from front-line staff to the chief executive should strive to meet and exceed service standards.

10.1. CUSTOMERS ARE YOUR BUSINESS

You may offer a quality, well-priced product, but if a customer receives inferior service before, during or after the sale, future sales may be lost. Providing superior customer service in today's competitive marketplace is crucial. Quite simply, customers are your business and lost sales through poor service means you will lose money. Long-term business success isn't just a matter of having the best products or the biggest advertising budget. It boils down to customer satisfaction.

Satisfied customers are motivated to return and buy again from the same business more often. Aim to make good service part of your business culture. Targets for service delivery and customer satisfaction should be included in the business plan and in employee job descriptions. Encourage employees to understand it's the customers who ultimately pay their wages. Customer complaints should also be welcomed. Customer feedback can help refine and improve products, services and all the operations of a business.

If you think implementing customer service is too costly or time-consuming, think again. It doesn't have to be. Walk in to any large bookshop and you will find a selection of practical 'how-to' guides on customer service that you can implement easily. Business Enterprise Centres also have resources and short courses to help you improve customer service.

Customers, and customer service. Both go hand-in-hand, and both are essential to the success of your business. Unfortunately, our research has shown us that many small businesses still see customer service as being too hard, too expensive and a luxury only the bigger end of town can afford. The Guide helps take some of the hard work out of providing good customer service by turning best practice customer service theory into easy-to-follow actions. It provides practical and affordable solutions for all businesses regardless of how big they are or what they do.

So that's it, no tricks or magic formulas, just practical advice and common business wisdom that will keep customers happy and your business healthy.

10.2. CUSTOMER CARE

Customer care is a crucial element of business success. Every contact your customers have with your business is an opportunity for you to improve your reputation with them and increase the likelihood of further sales. From your telephone manner to the efficiency of your order-fulfilment systems, almost every aspect of your business affects the way your customers view your business. But there are also specific programmes you can put in place to increase your levels of customer care.

We could go about our internal meetings without problems, set-up strategies that we like and understand, decide where the funds should go... life would be so easy.... No customer, no cry. Of course, that scenario conveniently forgets that it is the customer who pays our bills. There is no doubt that the customer should be at the centre of every business strategy. And yet it often seems as if focusing on them is an afterthought, a single paragraph in a business plan, nothing more.

Thinking about the customer is not a natural function of many businesses—or even marketing, even though the latter's reason for being is its understanding of the customer. After all, isn't marketers' favourite discussion about how well they understand the customer, often better than anyone else in the company? Unfortunately, even that is eroding. In today's fragmented business place, customer interaction and customer treatment could easily be managed by a branch manager, a Web site, a call system, a customer relationship manager or a customer relationship management (CRM) solution. If you add a touch of business analytics, you will soon realise that many marketers already have little impact on customers.

The complexity of delivery, the complexity of promoting to the right people, the complexity of business in general... have shown over and over again that businesses that strive have an understanding of their customer base that goes beyond products and demographics, beyond the marketing department.

10.3. DEALING WITH SOPHISTICATED CUSTOMER

Customers around the world have become more sophisticated. Today, they have the power to compare price, buy abroad, buy directly or online, travel more and shop more; and, even more important, they can complain to the right person. That sophistication is at a crossroads however. Today, the customer can no longer assume that companies will try to get his business.

When you are bombarded with irrelevant offers and other marketing messages, deciding to be a good customer is a life strategy. We have the right to select one brand and ask to be treated correctly. We have the right to put all our accounts into one bank and then ask to be treated well; if we don't, then we have nothing much to ask in return for our lack of commitment.

Marketing as a discipline has changed in the past 100 years, and not always for the better. Some of the marketing books from 60-plus years ago seem to have been more in touch with customers than the discipline is today. It also feels that marketers understood better their role in the growth of the business. Today's marketer is often so sophisticated than he or she has lost touch with the customers. Hidden behind research numbers and focus groups, the marketer often has a warped view of what customers' true behavior is really like. It's interesting to notice that analytics based on behavior is trying to regain that lost knowledge. While thankfully not all marketers are so remote, all should be careful of the "ivory tower" syndrome and ensure that they and their team get down into the trenches, where customers are voting with their credit card.

The role of the business owner in serving the customer cannot be ignored. While he or she might not always be right there with them, his or her beliefs and business philosophy will make a company either customer-centric or not. The danger lies in being, once more, too remote—in treating customers as numbers. If the business leader is not customer-centric, no amount of internal training or strategy will make the company focus on the customer.

In all fairness, their main role is, of course, to bring in business, so it might not seem fair to ask them to nurture a relationship. Can you imagine, however, a customer who sees a sales person only when the latter wants something? What are the mid- and long-term implications? Would this impact the overall company's brand? You bet it would, and most probably negatively.

Becoming a customer-centric organisation is no longer a strategic question, it's a vital necessity. You have to become one. If you don't, your competition will—and your customers will follow them. And while you can use all the technology you need to enable your business to be customer-centric, if your business philosophy favours something else, you will never achieve that goal.

10.4. DEALING WITH CUSTOMER COMPLAINTS

A business that provides quality products or services is seeking complete customer satisfaction. In situations where customer complaints occur, the complaint must be dealt with immediately and the cause of the complaint rectified. Some companies are not concerned with quality and often ignore complaints or deal with them dishonestly.

When the customer pays for a product or service, it is assumed that the product will work correctly or that the service received is as promised. Ideally, the customer will be satisfied, and there will be no complaints. If there is a problem, and the customer complains about it, the company should quickly answer the complaint and solve the customer's problem. This is often done through the company's customer service activity.

— *Special bonus*: To make sure the customer is completely satisfied, some companies will provide some special service or a reduced price on another product. This is done to assure the customer will come back for more business.

— *Price in customer service*: When a company sells a product or a provides a service, part of the pricing should include the cost of servicing a certain percentage of defective products or complaints.

— *Rectify problem*: The second thing a company should do upon receiving a complaint is to seek to rectify the problem.

— *Although a company hopes not to get complaints, they often can be blessing in disguise.* Sometimes problems can be caught and fixed before they cause serious negative feedback or even legal problems. It is in the company's best interest to solve any problems and try to make sure that they don't happen again.

— *Businesses that don't bother about satisfying their customers usually get more customer complaints.* Answering them can, of course, cost the company money. Some companies will try to mollify angry customers but many don't even bother.

Have you ever experienced poor service or purchased a defective product and complained about it, only to have your complaints fall on deaf ears? Many companies that have plenty of business feel they don't need to bother with complainers. These businesses become very independent, especially if they have a product or service in demand. Some continue to succeed, even though they ignore customer complaints, but many will pay the price of lost business and degraded reputation in the long run.

Satisfied customer: First of all, it will help to satisfy the customer, so you will get repeat business or referrals. In fact, in some cases, effectively dealing with a customer complaint can lead to a more loyal customer than others who may not complain or have problems.

Another benefit of dealing with complaints is that you can see weaknesses in your process or products that can be rectified. This will prevent possible future complaints or problems down the line. It is an effective form of customer feedback, although one you hope to eliminate.

For every formal complaint you receive, there may be 10 other customers who were dissatisfied and who felt like complaining, but who never did. Instead, they change brands and tell their friends of the dissatisfaction. It is said that an unhappy customer will tell 13 people about his or her dissatisfaction. That is not the type of word-of-mouth advertising you want. The company goal should be to get no complaints at all.

Quickly and properly solving customer complaints can help your business grow and prosper. Ignoring complaints or dealing with them in a dishonest manner can result in loss of business or even lawsuits.

10.5.1.Techniques to Dealing with Customers

1. Remember...you're in the people work business not the paper work business.

2. Make your customers (shoppers) feel important. They're essential to your business.

3. Greet every person that walks through your doors immediately. Make strangers feel as welcome as regular customers.

4. Say "How may I help you?" or "How may I be of service?" rather than "Can I help you?."..or even worse..."Did you want some help?"

5. The customer always comes first when it comes to your job priorities. A customer takes precedence over talking to other employees, arranging the lot or paperwork.

6. Don't talk "shop" business in front of customers. Don't take or make personal phone calls when you're serving a customer or when customers are in the immediate area. Don't talk around or over the top of customer's heads.

7. Accompany people to the right area or department rather than merely pointing and saying "It's over there."

8. When speaking to anyone about credit problems or any difficulty, politely take them away from the area of other customers to speak with them in a non-public area.

9. Use more creative wording than the tired phrase "Have a nice day!" Be more than a robot with your speech.

10. Make the leaving as pleasant as the greeting. Always say "Thank you. Please come back and see us again." or "We appreciate your business."

11. Send Thank-You notes for purchases and future business.

12. Ask that they call you if everything did not meet their satisfaction. You want then to tell you, not 10 other people.

13. Make follow-up calls after the sale. Answer any unanswered questions. This is the time you can correct any problems.

14. Put on your "customer glasses." Look at all aspects of your business front the perspective your customer sees. What can you do to improve it?

15. Be easily accessible for those with physical limitations.

SUGGESTED READINGS

Adair J. (1988). *Effective Leadership*. Pan Books. London.

Bank J. (1992). *The Essence of Total Quality Management*. Prentice Hall. UK.

Born G. (1994). *Process Management to Quality Improvement*. John Wiley. Chichester (UK).

Crosby P.B. (1984). *Quality Without Tears*. McGraw-Hill. New York.

Donald C. Gause. (1989). *Exploring Requirements: Quality Before Design*. Dorset House Publishing Company. Inco.

Feigenbaum A.V. (1951). *Total Quality Control*. McGraw Hill. London.

Garvin G.A. (1988). *Managing Quality - The Strategic Competitive Edge*. The Free Press (Macmillan). New York.

Gerald M. Weinberg. (2001). *An Introduction to General Systems Thinking*. Dorset House Publishing Company. Inco.

Hutchins D. (1990). *In Pursuit of Quality*. Pitman. London.

_____ . (1992). *Achieve Total Quality*. Director Books. Cambridge (UK).

Ishikawa K. (1969). *Company Wide Quality Control Activities in Japan*. International Conference on Quality Control. Tokyo.

Juran J. M. (1951). *Quality Control Handbook*. McGraw-Hill. New York.

_____ , and Gryna F.M. (1970). *Quality Planning and Analysis*. McGraw-Hill. New York.

Kinlaw D.C. (1992). *Continuous Improvement and Measurement for Total Quality - a team-based approach*. Pfieffer & Business One (USA).

Macdonald J. and Piggot J. (1990). *Global Quality: the new management culture*. Mercury Books. London.

Mastenbrock W. (1991). *Managing for Quality in the Service Sector*. Basil Blackwell. Oxford (UK).

Murphy J.A. (1992). *Quality in Practice*. Gill and MacMillan. Dublin.

Oakland J.S. (1998). *Total Quality Management - The route to improving performance*. Butterworth-Heinemann.

—————————— (2000). *TQM Text With Cases*. Butterworth-Heinemann.

Sarv Singh Soin. (1992). *Total Quality Control Essentials - key elements. methodologies and managing for success*. McGraw-Hill. New York.

Talley D.J. (1991). *Total Quality Management: performance and cost measures*. ASQC. Milwaukee (USA).

Zairi M. (1994). *Measuring Performance for Business Results*. Chapman and Hall. London.